Sam Shepard, Arthur Kopit,
and the Off Broadway Theater

Twayne's United States Authors Series

Warren French, Editor
Indiana University

TUSAS 432

Sam Shepard, Arthur Kopit, and the Off Broadway Theater

By Doris Auerbach

Fairleigh Dickinson University

Twayne Publishers · Boston

Sam Shepard, Arthur Kopit,
and the Off Broadway Theater

Doris Auerbach

Copyright © 1982 by G. K. Hall & Company
All Rights Reserved
Published by Twayne Publishers
A Division of G. K. Hall & Company
70 Lincoln Street
Boston, Massachusetts 02111

Book Production by John Amburg
Book Design by Barbara Anderson

Printed on permanent/durable acid-free
paper and bound in the United States of
America.

Library of Congress Cataloging in Publication Data

Auerbach, Doris.
Sam Shepard, Arthur Kopit,
and the Off Broadway theater.

(Twayne's United States authors series ;
TUSAS 432)
Bibliography: p. 138
Includes index.
    1. American drama—20th century—
History and criticism.
2. Shepard, Sam, 1943–   —Criticism and interpretation.
3. Kopit, Arthur L.—Criticism and interpretation.
4. Off-Broadway theater.   I. Title.   II. Series.
PS351.A9   1982   812'.54'09   82-11975
ISBN 0-8057-7371-1

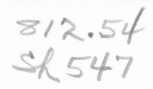
Contents

About the Author
Preface
Acknowledgments
Chronology

Chapter One
Sam Shephard: The Mythmaker   1

Chapter Two
The Early Plays   9

Chapter Three
Operation Sidewinder   22

Chapter Four
The Tooth of Crime   27

Chapter Five
The Way Home   42

Chapter Six
Buried Child   53

Chapter Seven
Speaking in Tongues   62

Chapter Eight
In the Bastard French Tradition: Arthur Kopit   66

Chapter Nine
*Oh Dad, Poor Dad, Mamma's Hung You
in the Closet and I'm Feelin' So Sad*   72

Chapter Ten
The Madhouse as Metaphor and
The Cherry Orchard Revisited   80

Chapter Eleven
A Myth Reconsidered: *Indians*   87

Chapter Twelve
The Mystery of Language   103

Chapter Thirteen
History of Off Broadway Theater   111

Notes and References   *129*
Selected Bibliography   *138*
Index   *143*

About the Author

Doris Auerbach is professor of German and chair of the Department of Foreign Languages and Literature at Fairleigh Dickinson University. She has the B.A. in English from Brooklyn College and the Ph.D. in German Literature from New York University. Her work on Brecht led her to explore the Off Broadway theater and two of its most talented contributors. She has also published in women's studies and gerontology.

Preface

On the surface, no two contemporary American playwrights have less in common, are less likely candidates for inclusion in the same book of criticism, than Sam Shepard and Arthur Kopit. In behavior and appearance Shepard epitomizes the West and its romantic involvement with American mythology, its avowed antiintellectualism, its limitless possibilities, its fecund creativity. Shepard came of age in the 1960s, and the language of his plays comes from the generation that grew up with television, science fiction, cool jazz, rock and drugs. Kopit couches his critique of American society in the literate idiom of an urbane eastern intellectual whose stance toward the American myth is skeptical and whose creative output is polished but not extensive.

Sam Shepard writes plays seemingly effortlessly in great quantity. He uses one-act plays like a painter used charcoal sketches, to approach an idea, a problem, a concern, from many different angles. Kopit, who has written but three major plays and four one-acters in the last twenty or so years, carefully considers an artistic and social concern, writes a carefully crafted statement, and moves slowly on toward the next one. Yet Shepard and Kopit share a communality of concerns for the meaning of the American myth, the evaluation and betrayal of the American dream, the fate of the American family, the precarious situation of the artist, the problems of identity, and perhaps most important, a fascination with the nature of language.

This book explores not only Shepard and Kopit's common interests, but the divergence of their style and their points of view, by a detailed study of their major works. While individual plays of both writers have received some critical consideration, no serious study of the playwrights' development has been undertaken. This book is an attempt to evaluate the work that these men have created up to now, recognizing the fact that neither one may as yet have reached the pinnacle of his creative potential.

Neither Shepard nor Kopit, nor most of today's serious theater practitioners, could have developed his craft had there not existed an alternative to the Broadway theater. The economics of the commercial stage do not permit the presentation of the experimental, the unpopular, the daring, the creative failures so vital to the young playwright. The noncommercial theater which has come to be called Off Broadway and Off-Off Broadway makes the development of such talents as Shepard and Kopit possible by permitting them to see their work on stage in front of a live audience. While noncommercial theater can be found from San Francisco to New Haven, its heart and soul remain the lofts and basements of New York that are Off Broadway and Off-Off Broadway. The last part of this book provides the reader with a short history of the development of the alternative, noncommercial theater of New York. The vitality of this theater depends on the creativity of playwrights who are unwilling to settle for the restraints that the Broadway theater imposes. Thus a healthy reciprocity between playwright and theater has been established that has helped create the viability of both Off Broadway and writers such as Shepard and Kopit.

Doris Auerbach

Fairleigh Dickinson University

Acknowledgments

The author wishes to express thanks to Fairleigh Dickinson University, whose granting of a sabbatical leave made the writing of this book possible; to Mr. Shepard, whose letters were of invaluable help in analyzing his work; to many colleagues, especially Dr. Lois Gordon, for their support; to Joan Beyer, who did far more than merely type the manuscript; and to my husband, George Auerbach, for his editorial suggestions and loving encouragement.

Chronology

Sam Shepard

1943 Sam Shepard Rogers, Jr., born at Fort Sheridan, Illinois.

1955 Family settled in California.

1961 Graduated Duarte, California, High School.

1962 Joined the Bishop's Company, a repertory company that toured throughout the country.

1963 Arrived in New York and changed his name to Sam Shepard.

1964 *Cowboys* and *Rock Garden* at the Theatre Genesis, New York.

1965 *Up to Thursday* at Theatre 65. *Dog* and *Rocking Chair* at La Mama Experimental Theatre Club. *Chicago* at Theatre Genesis in April. *Icarus' Mother* at Cafe Cino in November. *4-H Club* at Theatre 65.

1966 *Fourteen Hundred Thousand* at Firehouse Theatre, Minneapolis, later shown on National Educational Television. *Red Cross* at Judson Poet's Theatre.

1967 *La Turista* at American Place Theatre—awarded Obie. *Melodrama Play* at La Mama Experimental Theatre Club. *Cowboys No. 2* at Mark Taper Forum, Los Angeles. *Forensic and the Navigators* at Theatre Genesis—awarded Obie.

1968 Awarded Guggenheim Fellowship.

1969 Married O-Lan Johnson. *The Holy Ghostly* by La Mama Touring Company. *The Unseen Hand* at La Mama Experimental Theatre Club.

1970 Birth of a son, Jesse Mojo. *Operation Sidewinder* by Repertory Company of Lincoln Centre. *Shaved Splits* at La Mama Experimental Theatre Club.

1971 Moved to London. *Mad Dog Blues* at Theatre Genesis. *Cowboy*

Mouth, written with Patti Smith, British production at Edinburgh's Traverse Theatre; New York premiere at American Place Theatre. *Back Bog Beast Bait* at American Place Theatre.

1972   *The Tooth of Crime*—British production at Open Space Theatre, American premiere at Princeton University.

1973   *Blue Bitch*—B.B.C. Television.

1974   *Geography of a Horse Dreamer* at Theatre Upstairs, London. *Little Ocean* at Hampstead Theatre Club, London. Returned to California.

1975   *Action*, simultaneously opened at Magic Theatre in San Francisco and American Place Theatre in New York. Awarded Obie.

1976   *Angel City* at Magic Theatre, San Francisco. *Suicide in B Flat* at Yale Repertory Theatre. *Curse of the Starving Class* at New York Shakespeare Festival. Awarded Obie for best New American Play of the Season. Awarded Brandeis Creative Arts Medal.

1977   *Inacoma* at Magic Theatre in San Francisco.

1978   *Seduced* at American Place Theatre. *Buried Child* at Magic Theatre, San Francisco, East Coast premiere at Yale Repertory.

1979   Awarded Pulitzer Prize for *Buried Child*. *Tongues* at Magic Theatre in San Francisco. New York premiere at New York Shakespeare Festival.

Arthur J. Kopit

1937   Arthur J. Kopit born May 10 in New York City.

1955   Graduated Lawrence High School, Lawrence, Long Island, New York.

1957   *Questioning of Nick, Gemini, Don Juan in Texas, On the Runway of Life, You Never Know What's Coming Off Next* produced at Harvard.

1958   *Across the River and Into the Jungle* produced at Harvard. *To Dwell in a Place of Strangers*, Act I, published in *Harvard Advocate. Aubade* produced at Harvard.

1959   *Sing to Me Through Open Windows* produced at Harvard. Graduated Phi Beta Kappa. *Questioning of Nick* produced for television.

1960   Won Prize for Best Play for *Oh Dad, Poor Dad, Mamma's Hung You in the Closet and I'm Feeling So Sad*, Agassiz Production with help of a Rockefeller Grant—published by Hill & Wang.

1961   *Oh Dad, Poor Dad* produced in London.

1962   *Oh Dad, Poor Dad* produced in New York at the Phoenix Theater. Won the Vernon Rice Award and the Outer Circle Award.

1964   *Conquest of Everest* and *The Hero. The Day the Whores Came Out to Play Tennis* produced at Harvard.

1965   *Sing to Me Through Open Windows* produced in New York, directed by Joseph Chaikin. *The Day the Whores Came Out to Play Tennis and Other Plays* (book).

1967   Awarded a Guggenheim Fellowship.

1968   *Indians* produced in London and Washington. Received Rockefeller Fellowship. *An Incident in the Park* published in *Pardon Me Sir, But Is My Eye Hurting Your Elbow.*

1969   *Indians* produced in New York.

1971   National Institute of Arts and Letters Award. *Chamber Music* produced in London.

1972   *What Happened to the Thorne's House* produced in Peru, Vermont. *The Hero* produced in London.

1974   *The Questioning of Nick* produced in New York. National Endowment for the Arts Award. Weslyan University Center for Humanities Fellowship.

1976   *Sing to Me Through Open Windows*, revised version, done in London. Workshop production of *Secrets of the Rich* at the O'Neill Theatre Center, Wallingford, Connecticut.

1977   Kopit Festival at the Impossible Time Theater. *Wings* performed on National Public Radio "Ear Play." Awarded a Rockefeller Fellowship.

1978   *Wings* produced at Yale Repertory Theatre.

1979   *Wings* produced on Broadway.

Chapter One

Sam Shepard: The Mythmaker

The Major Themes of His Work

The title "mythmaker" has been as firmly affixed to Sam Shepard's name as a patronym. His name elicits this response in every review of his plays, in any reference to him in the popular media, and in the few scholarly articles that are beginning to be written about America's most prolific young playwright. By definition, a myth is an attempt to explain a phenomenon or a historical event while at the same time unfolding the world-view of a people—a very apt description of the work of a writer who has been called the most American of all our contemporary dramatists.

Sam Shepard's subject is simply this—America. The America about us, the American dream that has been betrayed, the American hero whose quest has become perverted, the American land which has become unproductive, sterile, and the American family which no longer nurtures its children—these are Shepard's themes. The American idiom of Shepard is the language of one young enough to have incorporated all of our modern transmitters of culture—radio, movies, phonograph records, TV—into his consciousness and speech from early childhood on. Since myths explain the world about us and the forms these explanations take are determined by the culture from which they emanate, it was natural for Shepard to use the images with which he had grown up. The cowboys, the prospectors, the Indians, the gangsters, the pop singers, the movie stars of popular culture became the building stones with which he created his vision of America.

It was inevitable that these mythic explanations would be applied to the writer himself. In a recent article, Shepard's words used to describe Bob Dylan were used to portray him: "Sam Shepard has invented himself. He's made himself up from scratch. That is from the things around him and inside him. Sam is the invention of his own mind."[1] If indeed Shepard, as perhaps all of us do, has invented himself, he has kept the invention as quiet as possible. He has been enigmatic about his personal life and fiercely protective of his privacy. The myth of the mysterious stranger whose origins may not be questioned is easily evoked. In a society where the artist is almost as rapidly consumed as his wares, this attitude has an element of healthy self-preservation about it. Although he continues to avoid interviews and reporters and has not left California since his return there in 1975, the fame brought on by the Pulitzer Prize he won in 1979 and his exposure as an actor in *Days of Heaven* and *Resurrection* have resulted in several magazine articles recently.

Beginnings

He was born in 1943 in Fort Sheridan, Illinois, while his army officer father was in Italy. He grew up as an army brat in South Dakota, Utah, Florida, and Guam, until the family settled in California in 1955. In an autobiographical sketch, he reminisced about his California adolescence:

I grew up on an avocado ranch in Duarte, California. I had 25 head of sheep and was a registered 4H club member. I became a thief at the Los Angeles County Fair where we used to steal goose eggs and goat's milk for breakfast. I was thrown in jail in Big Bear for giving the wife of the Chief of Police the finger. I rolled over four times in a Renault Dauphine while stoned on Benzedrine and landed right side up in a gas station, with nothing but the wind knocked out of me. I stole a car once in Pasadena and got away with it. I used to go to the Rose Parade and watch Leo Carillo and the Lone Ranger and Hoppalong Cassidy riding their horses on Orange Grove Boulevard. I went to the Pasadena Civic Auditorium to see the Beach Boys play and we'd get drunk and act real tough.[2]

In 1963 this modern Huck Finn joined the Bishop's Company Repertory Players and traveled throughout the United States performing in Christopher Fry plays and in an adaptation of Winnie-the-Pooh. After eight months of performing in church halls, he landed in

New York City and teamed up with his painter buddy Charles Mingus, Jr., son of the jazz musician. Together they moved to the East Village: "The world I was living in was the most interesting thing to me, and I thought the best thing I could do maybe would be to write about it."[3]

In order to support himself, he worked as a busboy at the Village Gate, where Charles was a waiter. He still has fond memories of those days where he got to hear the best jazz in New York, and got paid for it to boot. The staff of the Village Gate were mostly unemployed actors, directors, artists, and musicians, and Shepard met his first producer there, Ralph Cook, who was waiting tables. Cook also was trying to get the Theatre Genesis started, and when he was given space in St. Marks-in-the-Bouwerie Church, Shepard's one-act plays *Cowboys* and *Rock Garden* were among the new group's first offerings. Both these early plays deal with two themes which have continued to fascinate Shepard; in *Cowboys*, the search for the lost American hero, and in *Rock Garden*, the decline of the American family. The young writer almost packed up and returned to California when the first reviews came out. A rave review by the *Village Voice* critic, Michael Smith, turned the tide and brought audiences to see the new writer.

Culture, Consumerism, and Myth

Shepard himself cannot keep track of the number of plays he has written since then. Thirty of them, however, have been produced. In all of them, he explores his interest in the particular American underpinnings of his language, the unconscious foundations on which American cultural life rests. It is only through the use of the specific American idiom that he can perceive and recreate reality. "The cultural environment one is raised in predetermines a rhythmical relationship to the use of words. In this sense I can't be anything other than an American writer," he states.[4] Shepard, like most transmitters of unique vision, is struggling to maintain it in an era of overexposure to mass communication and mass culture. The French anthropologist Levi-Strauss calls this phenomenon "over-communication, the tendency to know exactly in one part of the world what is going on in all other parts."[5] In order for a culture to be itself, and produce something, he writes, that culture and its members must be convinced of their uniqueness. We are threatened by being consumers of everything and producers of nothing. How threatening this consumerism is to the artist Shepard expresses in *Angel City*: "How can I stay immune? How can I keep my distance from a machine like that?"[6] The over-stimulation brought about by the persistent onslaught of pop culture threatens not only a unified artistic vision but an integrated self as well.

Shepard's use of uniquely American mythic thinking is an attempt to turn away from the consumption of culture to the production of it. Using American myths to explain the world about him and to explore the causes of the current American malaise, he proceeds not like a modern scientist but like a witch doctor who relates illness to the world of myths. "Myths speak to everything all at once, especially the emotions," he writes in "Visualization, Language and the Inner Library"(55). The familiar American myths with which we have grown up have the power of evoking each other. In *The Mad Dog Blues*, Waco, for instance, calls up the image of Humphrey Bogart in *The Treasure of Sierra Madre*, and the allusion to Janis Joplin brings to mind the deaths of such other American culture heroes as Jimi Hendrix and James Dean. Even though dead, these, like the cowboys of our past, are alive within us.

How our uniquely American references work for us is shown partic-ularly well in a play like *The Mad Dog Blues*. Levi-Strauss considers one of the properties of myth that it can be observed under different transformations but understood only when comprehended in its totality. In *The Mad Dog Blues*, Yahoodi, during Kosmos and Mae West's imaginary trolley ride, relates his own childhood memory of a subway ride. This seeming non-sequitur reference to the world's indifference, which has little to do with the action on stage, can only be understood when the play as a whole has been experienced and the "myth" seen in its various guises. Thus Kosmos (Everyman) is trying to explain to Mae West his vision of her singing like Janis Joplin; but Mae is as indifferent to the dead Janis as the subway riders are to Yahoodi[7]—as in fact the world has always been indifferent to Yahoodi, whose name calls up the archetype of the Wandering Jew. Shepard's legendary figures from Marlene Dietrich to Captain Kidd to

Paul Bunyan are used again and again in this play to portray our
rootlessness and our materialism, shown by the search for the gold.
Kosmos and Yahoodi search for it in the hope that "with it we'll be
able to do anything, to go anywhere and be anyone we want to be"
(161), not realizing that this quest will turn out to be like the gold
itself just a sham, bags of useless bottle caps. To be "anybody" is in
fact to be nobody and to be "anywhere" is in fact to be nowhere. Thus
the subway description is only comprehended in its totality toward
the end of the play, when the stage directions read: "They all keep up
their search, calling out to each other across a vast expanse" (192).
The writer's threatened diffusion of vision is underlined by his
apprehension of being not somebody but anybody.

The Love of Logos

What makes Sam Shepard's work peculiarly his own is his use
of language. He came into the foreground of the American theater
scene when the written aspects of drama were being downplayed in
favor of ritual, performance, and the nonverbal. He brought the word
back into the theater when influential theoreticians such as Richard
Schechner were proclaiming that the end of written theater was upon
us. Shepard continues to believe in the real power of words which have
the ability to evoke visions in the eyes of the audience. Words, to
Shepard, are "living incantations"[8] which provide glimpses into the
total world of sensate experience. "They are tools of imagery in motion,"[9]
he writes. Above all, they are the writer's instruments for penetrating
into another world, a world behind the form; they are the means by
which he can make leaps into the unknown, and discover what Emily
Dickinson called "ourself behind ourself concealed." According to
Shepard, "There's only so much I can do with appearance. Change the
costume, add a new character, change the lights, bring in objects,
shift the set, but language is always hovering right in there, ready to
move faster and more effectively than all the rest of it put together.
It's like pulling out a .38 when someone faces you with a knife."[10]
The heart of theatrical experience for Shepard is language. "The
organization of living, breathing words as they hit the air between the
actor, and the audience actually possesses the power to change our

chemistry."[11] Shepard used these words in a process he calls note-taking on an event that takes place inside him. The characters in his plays appear to him three-dimensionally and speak. The plays do not develop from ideas, but "Ideas emerge from plays—not the other way around."[12] They develop from the impulse to see something happen on stage. This permits him to "play" with the characters, the situation, the words. The process of note-taking, or play-writing, requires constant new expression to describe essentially foreign, unexplored countries. The writer must learn to mold a new language, a new experience into form.

Sam Shepard has been called a lover of logos who in his plays recreates the lost American idioms of the American mythic West, part TV, part legend, part Southwest Mountain, part Los Angeles. "This hillbilly language of Shepard, this beautiful American tongue is still to be heard in great parts of the country, in the towns, on the road."[13] But Shepard's people speak often as if they stepped out of the TV or movie screen or the radio, as if the reality of mass communication were "realer" to them than life. The culture he portrays is one of manipulated passivity, as the poet Adrienne Rich calls it, whose mirror image is violence.

In Shepard plays, the downfall of the hero can sometimes be brought about by words alone—a hero is defeated by an opponent whose language has greater power to overcome passivity and initiate action. Hoss in *The Tooth of Crime* is routed by Crow's superior verbal force, triumphing over the hero, who has become paralyzed into inaction. Words themselves become the metaphor for action and the tools for influencing and controlling the world about us. They are the means by which we can counteract the loaded messages of the mass media.

Shepard has often objected to the tendency of critics to overemphasize the intellectual aspects of playwriting: "In general for me the intellect must serve the life of *experience* in all my work. It makes no sense to me to conceptualize a piece of work just because the experiencing of it is mysterious. . . . By deeply submerging oneself into the predicament, come all the questions, all the language, all the form. Not from the head. The head, at best, can only make up theories and theories don't hold water if experience defies them."[14] This statement evokes the image of Brecht, one of Shepard's favorite writers, who in *The Threepenny Opera* has Peachum sing:

> A man lives by his head.
> That head will not suffice.
> Just try it: you will find your head
> Will scarce support two lice. [15]

The problem of overemphasizing the idea and the concept of a play is that it invariably leaves out the body and the emotions, Shepard claims. His theater is visceral theater, speaking to the audience on an emotional level that goes beyond what he calls "meaning." His words are underscored and heightened by his use of music. He believes that music can reach an audience more immediately and deeply than gesture and language. Music has been as integral part of many of Shepard's plays, most notably: *The Tooth of Crime*, *Angel City*, *The Mad Dog Blues*, *Cowboy Mouth*, *Suicide in B Flat*, and *Tongues*. Not since Brecht has a dramatist used music as such an integral part of the play. The primary appeal of music to the senses has been amply commented upon. Its relationship to the structure of myth, which Levi-Strauss has explored, ties it neatly to Shepard's fascination with myths which like music "speak to everything at once, especially the emotions." [16]

The Dream Betrayed

The theme to which Shepard returns again and again in his plays is the betrayal of the American dream that promised fulfillment and nourishment for all. The land that no longer bears fruit and the hunger that cannot be stilled cry out to us from Shepard's stage. His characters seem obsessed by food. In some plays such as *Curse of the Starving Class* and *Buried Child*, the stage is littered by bushels of produce. In one of his latest works, the two one-act plays that make up *Tongues*, the protagonist talks about a hunger that cannot be appeased: "I am famished . . . nothing I ate could satisfy this hunger I'm having right now."

The betrayed American dream, void of fruitfulness and satisfaction, at whose core is violence, is evoked in all of Shepard's plays.

They are void also of human feeling. He portrays a man's world—brutal and cold, where adversaries struggle endlessly for domination and power over each other. The female characters are of no help to the protagonists, for they are mere macho fantasies of familiar female stereotypes, castrating mothers and devouring sex goddesses, who offer no hope for transcendence. The only love portrayed is the ambivalent relationship between buddies, such as Yahoodi and Kosmos in *The Mad Dog Blues*. Shepard is dealing here with another pervasive American myth: "The man on the run, harried into the forest, and out to sea, down the river and into combat—anywhere to avoid 'civilization,' which is to say the confrontation of a man and a woman."[17] Shepard's heroes are wanderers without protection, without mothers, doomed without the mediating feminine principle to clash eternally on a darkling plain. Shepard paints our American world as one obsessed by violence and embarrassed before love, a world which becomes for lack of Eros dedicated to Thanatos.

A recent article suggested that Shepard's protagonists were sons continually searching for an accepting father.[18] I would suggest that even more than acceptance from a father, they are searching for a mother whose nurturance would make the world fruitful again.

Chapter Two
The Early Plays

The Rock Garden

Cowboys and *The Rock Garden* opened on October 16, 1964, at Ralph Cook's new Theatre Genesis. It was, as Shepard recollects, "a sort of Village Gate company."[1] The opening was not an unqualified success. Shepard was accused of imitating Beckett, and "all these guys [reviewers] said it was a bunch of shit."[2] Due to one enthusiastic review in the *Village Voice*, however, people came to hear this new voice in the American theater. The first play, *Cowboys*, is now lost, but the second one-acter on the bill, *The Rock Garden*, is still considered by Shepard to be one of his better plays. Recently he quite candidly dubbed it a better-constructed play than some of his more mature work such as *Curse of the Starving Class*.[3] The play caused somewhat of a scandal in New York, which probably led to the inclusion of its last scene in the sensational revue *Oh, Calcutta!* The royalties from this helped to keep Shepard financially afloat in several lean periods. He reminisced about it in an interview in a British theater journal:

> *Rock Garden* is about leaving my mom and dad. It happens in two scenes. In the first scene the mother is lying in bed ill while the son is sitting on a chair, and she is talking about the special kind of cookie that she makes, which is marshmallow on salt crackers melted under the oven. It's called "angels on horseback," and she has a monologue about it. And then the father arrives in the second scene. The boy doesn't say anything, he's just sitting in this chair, and the father starts to talk about painting the fence around the house, and there's a monologue about that in the course of which the boy keeps dropping off to sleep and falling off his chair. Finally the boy has a monologue about orgasm that goes on for a couple of pages and ends in his coming all over the place, and then the father falls off the chair.[4]

In this very early one-act play, Shepard plays his first variation on the theme of the breakdown of the American family. The play is really

9

devoid of dialogue; in the form of baroque opera, the three characters sing their arias to the audience, not to each other. There is no verbal communication at all among them. In both its form and content it was a play for its time—the mid-1960s, when the first cracks in the complacency of American society were beginning to become very obvious. Michael Allen of St. Mark's Church defended the play against those critics who questioned the propriety of producing such a play in a church, and articulated one of the first "make-love-not-war" pleas: "The play is dominated to the end by the parents whose conversation is filled with subtle sexual imagery, hypocritically disguised. The boy is franker than they are, that's all, and maybe he thinks sex is not evil. I believe this whole generation of young people is saying to us in effect, 'Look, you use beautiful words and do ugly things; we'll take ugly words and make beauty of them!' "[5]

The Prolific Period

Between 1964 and 1969, Sam Shepard had fourteen plays produced in New York; and he had written countless more. He laconically recalls that he got into the habit of writing because "there was nothing else to do."[6] He wrote very quickly. "The stuff would just come out and I wasn't really trying to shape it or make it into a big thing."[7] What he was doing was learning his craft in the only way he knew—by writing plays. The young Shepard marveled that writers take "reams of notes before they ever go into the thing, but with me I write plays before I go into something else."[8] He remembers that "I used to be dead set against rewriting on any level. My attitude was that if the play had faults, those faults were part and parcel of the entire process, and that any attempt to correct them was cheating. Like a sculptor sneaking out in the night with his chisel and chipping little pieces off his work and gluing them back on."[9] The youthful arrogance slowly evolved into the more humble attitude of the professional: "After a while this 'holy-art' concept began to crumble. It was no longer a case of 'correcting,' as though I was involved with some kind of definitive term paper. I began to see that the living outcome (the production) always demanded a different kind of attention than the written form it sprang from."[10]

Sam Shepard became part of the whole Off-Off Broadway scene that was just beginning to be important in the New York theater. His plays were produced at such now legendary theaters as the Theater 65, La Mama, Cafe Cino, the Judson Poets' Theatre, and the American Place Theatre. He recollects it being "a very exciting time" full of the sense of something going on. The excitement made up for the lack of monetary reward. He made no money at all from the early plays: "There wasn't any money at all, until the grants started coming in from Ford and Rockefeller and all these places that were supporting the theatres because of the publicity they started getting. Then they began to pay the actors and playwrights—but it wasn't much, $100 for five weeks' work or something."[11] It may have been the lack of money that kept Shepard from considering writing a job, but aside from that consideration, "I never thought of it as my job, because it was something that made me feel more relaxed, whereas I always thought of jobs as something that made you feel less alive—you know, the thing of working ten hours a day cleaning horse shit out of a stable."[12]

Theater 65 presented *Up To Thursday* in February 1965. According to Shepard, who does not remember the play kindly, it "was a bad exercise in absurdity. This kid is sleeping in an American flag, he's only wearing a jockstrap or something, and there's four people on stage who keep shifting their legs, talking. I can't remember it very well—it was a terrible play, really."[13] This play has never been published; neither has *Dog* nor *Rocking Chair*, which also appeared at La Mama in February 1965. Shepard was not only trying out all kinds of new subjects, techniques, and language, but he was also tuning into the feelings and concerns of the young of the 1960s. He recalls that "*Dog* was about a black guy—which later I found out it was uncool for a white to write about in America. It was about a black guy on a park bench, a sort of 'Zoo Story' type of play."[14] The second half of the double bill failed even more miserably in the writer's memory. "I don't even remember *Rocking Chair*, except it was about somebody in a rocking chair."[15]

Chicago

Chicago, which opened at the Theatre Genesis in April 1965, and which Shepard recalls as having been written in one day, begins an exploration of the nature of commitment and freedom, a theme which appears again and again in Shepard's later works. As in many of his plays, bizarre as they often are, the action of *Chicago* unfolds against a familiar domestic background—a man, Stu, is taking a bath, and his girl friend Joy is making biscuits. As the play begins a voice recites the Gettysburg Address while a policeman pounds the curtain with his stick. As Joy wonders on and off stage, occasionally joining Stu in the tub, her friends arrive to see her off to begin a new job. As she walks across the stage pulling a wagonload full of her luggage, her friends sit down on the edge of the stage and cast their fishing lines into the audience. Stu delivers a long monologue, and the play ends with the policeman knocking three times again.

Stu, who spends most of the play in the tub, discourses at great lengths about fish and fishermen. He sees a symbiotic relationship between the two, remarking, "You're both hung up." According to R. A. Davis, this dependency has other obvious parallels to our society: "Once either, fish or fisherman, accepts the economically reciprocal system, he loses something of his freedom. And the fish or worker, while gaining necessities such as food, also stands to lose his life or individuality on the hook."[16] Joy, who leaves to begin a new job, and the friends who sit fishing, have accepted this societal arrangement. Stu, in his bathtub, delivers his soliloquy on the joys of breathing, which he seems to equate with human freedom. Yet he, too, is looking for a relationship; he encourages the audience to join him in a spiritual, not material, symbiosis. Shepard brings this play into the realm of mid-1960s American politics by setting up the antithesis of the idealism of the Gettysburg Address and the policeman's stick.

Icarus's Mother

When in November 1965 Shepard's seventh play, *Icarus's Mother*, was presented by the Cafe Cino, the critics began to pay attention to this prolific young writer. In one of the most prestigious journals, the *Saturday Review*, reviewer Robert Shayon wrote that the audience had to "enter into a guessing game with the author, trying to decipher the symbolism that one suspects is latent under the deceptive simplicity of the apparent content."[17] Shepard chose the most everyday kind of backdrop for this "guessing game." Five young people are having a picnic on the Fourth of July; as the curtain rises, the stage directions tell us they are lying on their backs, "belching at random," and waiting for the fireworks to begin. A sense of outside threat is introduced with the discussion of a plane which circles overhead and symbolizes the menace which is soon to rupture the pastoral calm. Nothing much happens in the play; the characters wander off singly or in pairs, talking about the mysterious plane, until the plane is described as having crashed, and fireworks take place. The pilot, who observes the characters on earth, and the people who look up at the aviator are the two poles between which the tension of the play develops. The pilot soaring above is a symbol of spiritual heights, a man who separates himself from the earthbound creatures below but who is also constantly drawn down to earth by his own sexuality. The two girls, Pat and Jill, have gone down the beach; as they squatted on the sand to pee, the plane flew quite low. The girls waved at the pilot, took off their pants, and danced for him, as he did gyrations and flips. The pilot then climbs up to 40,000 feet and writes $E = mc^2$ in the sky. Frank describes the crash as the Fourth of July fireworks orchestrate his account. The pilot is literally burning up his energy. He shows if off to the two girls by climbing as high as he can and then diving down like Icarus, becoming earthbound again. A critic has suggested that the whole play can be seen as a symbolic act of sexual intercourse—the pilot's position above the earth, his plunge downward, and his death in a tremendous explosion or fireworks.[18] To Howard and Bill, the pilot, the man who soars above the herd, is both threatening and tantalizing. They shout threats up at him, but they try to attract his attention with smoke signals from the barbecue in an attempt to communicate with someone beyond their conventional existence. Frank is inspired by him to find a perfect beach, away from the dirt and clutter. The two girls seem to express all that which keeps man from his spiritual goals and draws him back down to earth. Icarus's father may have taught him to fly and soar, but his mother pulled him back down to earth and death.

When the play was performed in London in 1970, it was seen in much more political terms; in an interview in a British journal,

Shepard relates the setting of *Icarus's Mother* directly to the American roots for which he was searching:

I was in Wisconsin, in Milwaukee, and for the Fourth of July we have this celebration—fireworks and all that kind of stuff—and I was in this park with these people, with this display going on. You begin to have a feeling of this historical thing being played out in contemporary terms—I didn't even know what the Fourth of July meant, really, but there was this celebration taking place, with explosions. One of the weird things about being an American now, though I haven't been there much lately, is that you don't have any connection with the past, with what history means. So you can be there celebrating the Fourth of July, but all you know is that things are exploding in the sky. And then you've got this emotional thing that goes a long way back, which creates a certain kind of chaos, a kind of terror, you don't know what the fuck is going on. It's really hard to grab the whole experience.[19]

By leaving the United States, Sam Shepard was eventually able to find the distance which he needed in order to discover his own roots. But at the end of 1965 he was still in New York with *4H Club* at the Theatre 65. The title comments ironically on the images that it evokes and the scenes which it describes. Three men are trapped in a squalid urban setting and act out the meaninglessness of their lives in the gratuitous violence of killing rats. A critic suggested that it was reminiscent of "Beckett's reified metaphors and LeRoi Jones's urban cul-de-sacs."[20]

By early 1966, Sam Shepard's name had begun to be known outside of New York, and *Fourteen Hundred Thousand* was presented by the Firehouse Theatre of Minneapolis and subsequently shown on NET-TV, "so my mother got to see it."[21] It is a somewhat puzzling play about someone building bookcases. A British critic suggested to Shepard that the play "changes directions two thirds of the way through—there's this play about building a bookshelf, and this other play about a linear city."[22] Shepard good-naturedly agreed with this critique: "Yeah, I had a long talk with an architect before I wrote that play, and stuck that into it. I was very interested in the idea of the linear city, because it struck me as being a strong visual conception as opposed to radial cities—the idea of having a whole country, especially like America, with these lines cutting across them."[23]

Red Cross

Red Cross, which was produced by the Judson Poets' Theatre and directed by Jacques Levy, was included in a collection called *The New Underground Theatre*. The editor of the anthology characterized *Red Cross* as "a prime example of the underground school's manic monologue. The characters take turns in spinning intriguing whirls of imaginative fancy in obsessively incongruous circumstances."[24] While the play received more than its share of attention, it was also characterized as "absolutely unrecommendable," by one disgruntled, confused reviewer,[25] who asked petulantly what was eating the main character anyway. On the surface what was eating him was crab lice that had infected his entire body. He complains of them at length to Carol, with whom he shares a mountain cabin. Carol, in turn, is plagued by all kinds of pains in the head. Before she leaves to get groceries, she delivers a monologue describing her nightmare of her head falling off. Her imagery in painting this catastrophic event is reminiscent of Frank's description of the plane crash in *Icarus's Mother*. When the maid arrives to change the sheets, Jim tries to teach her how to swim. This gives him the opportunity to talk at length about swimming and breathing in an "aria" reminiscent of Stu's discourse on breathing in *Chicago*. The maid finally leaves, and Carol returns, complaining of being covered by little bugs. When Jim turns to face her and the audience, there is a stream of blood running down his forehead. The stage directions call for the set and costumes to be all white, thus making the cabin in the woods a Red Cross survival station. But Jim has infected Carol with crabs, and at the end of the play, he seems to be bleeding from invisible head wounds, acting out Carol's vision of her head falling off. It is one of Shepard's most pessimistic plays, expressing all the uneasiness of the young in the mid-1960s. There seems to be no first aid available to ease the pervading American malaise.

La Turista

La Turista was something of a landmark for Shepard. It was his first full-length play; it was the first written outside the United States, and it was "the first play I ever rewrote, under the urging of Jacques Levy, who directed it."[26] He recalls that in the second week of rehearsals for the American Place Theater's production, he walked in with a new second act:

That was the first taste I got of regarding theatre as an ongoing process. I could feel the whole evolution of that play from a tiny sweltering hotel in the Yucatan, half-wasted with the trots, to a full-blown production in New York City. Most of the writing in that piece was hatched from a semidelirious state of severe dysentery. What the Mexicans call "La Turista" or "Montezuma's Revenge." In that state any writing I could manage seemed valid, no matter how incoherent it might seem to an outside eye. Once it hit the stage in rehearsal and I was back to a fairly healthy physical condition, the whole thing seemed filled with an overriding self-pity. The new second act came more from desperation than anything else.[27]

Despite the new second act, the play still suffers from being overburdened with too many concerns and issues, and too many experimental techniques. It is important, for in it Shepard articulates his fascination with myths and mythic roles whose primal force still pervades our so-called scientific age. The never-ending battle between father and son can be seen clearly in the relationship between the tourist Kent, who is half-dead with "La Turista," and the young Mexican boy, who usurps Kent's bed and replaces him sexually. Kent realizes the danger modern man is in when he puts his mind in the controlling position and neglects his body. "But the mind ain't nothing without the old body tagging along behind him to follow things through."[28] This is a point of view that Shepard has steadfastly continued to defend.

The characters in *La Turista* continually shift identities, skin color, and their spatial and temporal realities. While this can be explained on a mundane level by the writer's physical condition, it also "dramatizes the force of an unconscious which constantly threatens to break through the conventional fabric of personal and social existence."[29]

The theme that unconscious drives present a menace to an ordered existence brings the playwright close to the concerns of the young Brecht. This common concern will manifest itself more strongly in Shepard's later play, *The Tooth of Crime.*

The two young Americans in *La Turista* are named after two popular brands of cigarettes, and Shepard plays with the well-known advertising slogans in order to delineate his characters. Kent is a young man who experiences life in a civilization that "filters out" the primal and elemental aspects of life; Salem exemplifies "springtime freshness," but her words and actions belie the innocence and optimism implied.

The rewritten second act of *La Turista* urges the audience to compare and contrast it with what they have seen in the first act, and reflect upon it. The nature of the disease Kent suffers from is related to the general state of health of American society, which seems as immune to the cure of the witch doctors of the first act as to that of the doctors in Act II, who are dressed in Civil War uniforms. The American myths of the frontier "Doc" are no longer viable, can no longer help modern man. At the end of the play, Kent has been turned into a Frankenstein-like creature, seemingly healthy but definitely no longer human. *La Turista* is the first play in which Shepard suggests that genuine human existence is hard put to survive in our society.

Shepard returned to the writing of one-act plays after *La Turista*, as he has after the production of all his full-length works. In an article in *Theater* in the spring of 1978, more than ten years after the production of this first full-length play, Shepard rebels against the notion that only long plays can "serve as proof" of a playwright's worth. He continues to resent the idea that "the public deserves to get its money's worth and that this value lies in length rather than in quality, or that only in length can there be any quality."[30]

In May 1967, the first of Shepard's plays to utilize rock music both as content and as structural element, *Melodrama Play*, opened at La Mama Experimental Theatre Club, directed by Tom O'Horgan. Several elements that Shepard expresses in more mature works surface in this play. These are the rivalry between brothers, Duke and Drake; our society's exploitation of the creative artist—first Duke, and then

Drake is forced to write hit tunes under armed guard; the nature of power—its source and its style. Here, as eventually in *The Tooth of Crime* and *Suicide in B Flat*, a musical scene is used as a metaphor for society. In *Melodrama Play* Shepard begins to explore the connection between the creative drive and the lust for power—and the violence lying just below the surface of both.

Cowboys No. 2

In November 1967, the Mark Taper Forum in Los Angeles premiered *Cowboys No. 2*, the revised version of Shepard's first play. It was the shortest play that he had written, and the one that permitted him to explore most fully his fascination with our mythic past. He does so in this play by permitting his characters to role-play the Indians, "old-timers," and cowboys of our common imagination. In a technique strongly reminiscent of Brecht's, Shepard requires his actors to create in their imaginations and the imagination of the audience "those film sequences that inspire children to play Cowboys and Indians."[31] Kenneth Chubb, the English director of several of Shepard's plays, noted that the actor had to "throw himself into the role with childlike abandon and great intensity. But in the same way that a child can stop in the middle of a game and be himself, so an actor playing a man playing an 'old-timer' being attacked by Indians must be able to stop at any time and be the man or the actor."[32] According to Shepard, at this time he had not yet read Brecht, but he had always been drawn to the "play" aspect of the theater. As he stated succinctly in his article in the *Drama Review*: "The reason I began writing plays was the hope of extending the sensation of play (as in 'kid') on into adult life. If 'play' becomes 'labor,' why play?"[33]

In *Cowboys No. 2* the two young men, Chet and Stu, competitively play with these images, each trying to top the other in the impersonation. Here too Shepard introduces a metaphor with which he is still successfully working: hunger, which becomes extended in such later plays as *Curse of the Starving Class*, *Buried Child*, and *Tongues* into spiritual starvation. In *Cowboys No. 2* Stu and Chet reminisce about breakfast food and "morning" hunger—the hunger of the young that expects fulfillment. But this game ends with an image of death, as the land, "buried under luxuries, both useful ones like schools, and useless ones like peacocks,"[34] no longer nourishes its young. In this play Shepard again works with one of his favorite myths—the cowboy buddies, the one relationship that a man can count on.

Forensic and the Navigators

As the horrors of the Vietnam conflict became more and more disruptive to American society, Shepard's plays began to take on a more and more political tone. In *Forensic and the Navigators*, directed by Ralph Cook at the Theatre Genesis in December 1967, the possibilities of revolution are explored. In *Cowboys No. 2* he sounded the first of many warnings against the rape of the land by overmechanization. In *Forensic and the Navigators* he expresses the concerns of the young for successfully effecting political change against a system that is becoming evermore menacing. The three protagonists—Emmet and Forensic, dressed as Cowboy and Indian, and Olan, a girl—are involved in an attempt to blow up some government building. Their antagonists, called the Exterminators, are almost robotlike agents with no clear sense of purpose. Both the conspirators and the Exterminators are destroyed at the end of the play by a cloud of colored gas which blurs their identities before killing them. It seems clear that the heroes of our past have little chance against the nameless menace of impersonal authority. The female lead in the play is named for the young actress whom Shepard met and married at that time.

The Holy Ghostly

The Holy Ghostly, which Tom O'Horgan directed for La Mama's New Troupe in 1969, is a play that combines elements that directly foreshadow Shepard's more mature works. Complementing the central image of the Old West is an ever-increasing sense of violence, mirroring the ever-increasing violence of American society. In *The Holy Ghostly* Shepard also introduces the eternal struggle between father and son, which was to become one of the themes of both *The Tooth of Crime* and *Buried Child*. The son in *The Holy Ghostly* is a "cool" cowboy named Ice, who comes home to confront the eternal father,

"Pop," apparently to kill him and usurp his power. Before Ice is able to accomplish this, Pop scores some palpable hits, mocking the identity Ice has chosen as a "dressed-up hillbilly." Ice apparently "cools" Pop after the old man calls Ice's elaborate telling of the creation as "hogwash," thus impugning the son's power as an artist. But Pop rises again before the end of the play, and his corpse debunks his death scene. The stage directions then read: "He picks up the corpse, holds it over his head and spins it around in circles, then throws it into the fire. The drums and bells increase, the flames flicker all over the audience. The whole theatre is consumed in flames as Pop screams over and over and dances in the fire: BURN!BURN!BURN! BURN!"[35] The message is clear: The father, the authority figure, is not about to relinquish control to the Son peacefully. It will take a cataclysmic event, a revolution, before it will come about. Shepard was filling his plays with ever more styles and myths; the discipline and spareness of the more mature plays were still to come.

The Unseen Hand

The Unseen Hand, which opened at the La Mama in December 1969, received more critical attention in the United States after its 1973 London production. It was then characterized as "a hallucination based on fact."[36] The play is set in Shepard's native California. A banged-up '56 Chevy BelAir dominates the stage adjacent to a billboard of a smiling cowboy welcoming visitors to Azusa (Everything from A to Z in the U.S.A.). The plot revolves around the efforts of Willie to escape from the Hand, which squeezes and contracts his brain whenever he tries to "think beyond a certain circumference." The characters are drawn from the myths of our past—the old gunslingers and train robbers—and the media constructs of the present—science fictions and outer space. The old heroes are no longer viable; they have lost their function. The train robbers sadly realize that "they ain't no trains no more." What lifts the play above a somewhat confusing plot involving electronic transformations, the country of Nogoland, and a bare-assed cheerleader are words like these sung to a rock tune: "I love the Junior Chamber of Commerce, and the Kiwanis, and the Safari Shopping Center and the Freeway and the Bank of America and the Donut Shoppes and the Miniature Golf Course and setting off cherry bombs and my mom. . . ."[37] By this time, the end of 1969, Shepard was beginning to get some recognition in the popular press. The phenomenon frightened him. As he told an interviewer, he cherished his invisibility: "I prefer it that way. It's like the primitive feeling that if they take your photograph, your soul gets stolen. When someone's work becomes too popular you lose something."[38]

Chapter Three
Operation Sidewinder

The First Act

In the spring of 1970, Shepard's anonymity was to be shattered when *Operation Sidewinder*, still his most ambitious undertaking, opened at Lincoln Center's Beaumont Repertory Theatre as part of its season of American plays. The grandiose nature of the play demands both a large stage and a large house. It calls for a cast of seventeen men and four women in named parts, as well as fifteen unnamed Indians. It also requires such props as a six-foot-long mechanical snake with flashing eyes, a VW on a hydraulic lift, a '57 Chevy at a hot dog stand, a cave equipped for an Indian ceremony, including dozens of snakes, to say nothing of a rock band. Clearly, it was an undertaking that could not have been presented on the small stages of Off-Off Broadway.

Shepard introduces all the main characters of the play in the first act; all of these are searching for a change from an unbearable present. The Sidewinder is a computer in the shape of a six-foot-long sidewinder rattlesnake. It has escaped from the nearby air-force base, Fort George, and is roaming the desert. It has been created by a Dr. Strangelove type of mad, invalided scientist called Dr. Vector, to be the ultimate technological achievement with which man is to reach extraterrestrial consciousness. Onto the stage wander two typical middle-class tourists: the man, Dukie, has a "fancy-looking movie camera, straw cowboy hat, open shirt, hairy chest, and Bermuda shorts and Hush Puppies; Honey, his wife, is a typical macho dream figure of a woman, "a very sexy chick with long blond hair, tight pants, high heels," whose daydreams center around becoming a movie star. While the two tourists attempt to photograph the Sidewinder, the snake grabs Honey and wraps itself around her. The band plays a song that underlines the implicit sexuality of the snake's embrace: "Everytime I see you wanna do it girl/Rightout in the street

22

I wanna do it girl." Dukie runs off to get help and encounters the Young Man, who is getting his VW repaired by a mechanic. The Young Man, the "hero" of the play, is described as having "long blond hair down to his shoulders, a bright purple T shirt, tight leather pants and bare feet" (115). [1] He bears an amazing resemblance to photographs of Sam Shepard taken at the time. The Young Man shoots both Dukie and the mechanic when their conversation about the trapped Honey interrupts the work on his VW. He seems to be completely oblivious to the meaning of death, so strung-out on drugs that he reacts to the shooting of the two in a totally aloof manner. It is the same attitude that millions of Americans were taking as they watched the death agony of Vietnam in the comfort of their living rooms.

The Young Man has been hired by a group of black revolutionaries who hope to gain power by drugging the drinking water of Fort George, leaving the stoned pilots unable to protect the United States Government.

In the meantime, Honey reaches orgasm in the coils of the Side-winder computer, while Billie, the prototype of the Old Prospector, oblivious to Honey's danger, rambles on spinning yarns of the Old West. He is the go-between in the revolutionaries' plot, putting the Young Man in touch with the half-breed Indian Renegade, Mickey Free, who in exchange for handguns is to put the drugs into the reservoir. When the Young Man comes on stage to deliver the guns, he completely ignores Honey's plight. To Billie's question, "What about the lady?" he answers simply, "She has nothing to do with me" (123) and leaves. Billie leaves the stage singing "A beautiful bird in a gilded cage," an ironic comment on Honey in the coils of the Sidewinder. The prevalent disaffection is underlined by the band's singing a song entitled "Generalonely" (124).

The "Establishment" is introduced to the audience in the next scene by two drunken air-force officers who talk at length about hunting dogs with all the sympathy that they, at least in the opinion of the young in the late 1960s, seldom showed toward people. Honey is finally freed from the Sidewinder's embrace by Mickey Free, who severs the snake's head. The Young Man re-enters in order to give Mickey the dope with which to poison the reservoir. He notices the no-longer-trapped Honey and remarks, "I see you're free now. Why don't you split?" (129). Shortly thereafter, however, he enlists her help so he can shoot-up. The young, hooked on drugs and enmeshed in a mechanized society that brings about almost total lack of emotion, are neither free nor able to split the scene. Ironically using the body of the Sidewinder computer as a tourniquet, he finds the vein to inject. After Honey also gets her fix, the rock band, like the chorus in a Greek tragedy or the singer in a Brecht play commenting on the action on stage, sings about the magic of the drug experience in "Euphoria" (134).

In a scene strongly influenced by Kubrick's *Dr. Strangelove*, Dr. Vector confesses that he has let the Sidewinder computer escape so "it can be free," so its rhythmic movements can be studied in relationship to the movements of the planets and flight patterns of UFOs. The epitome of the mad scientist, Vector envisions "a form of intelligence which being triggered from the mind of man, would eventually, if allowed to exist on its own, transcend the barriers of human thought and penetrate an extraterrestrial consciousness" (142).

Still turned on, the Young Man confides his belief in magic to Honey—the magic of human warmth and friendship, which "made me feel free, my mind was lifting up in flight" (145). But what he feels most is oppressed and betrayed. He voices the profound disillusionment of the young in the wake of the 1968 presidential campaign: "The election oppression. Nixon, Wallace, Humphrey. The headline oppression every morning with one of their names on it. The radio news broadcast, TV oppression. And every other advertisement with their names and faces and voices and haircuts and suits and collars and ties and lies. And I was all set to watch "Mission Impossible" when Humphrey's flabby face shows up for another hour's alienation session" (145).

The young are pleading for "something soft, something human, something different, something real, something—so we can believe again" (145). But there is no answer coming, and what the Young Man fears the most is the disillusionment of his generation, "And the oppression of my fellow students becoming depressed. Depressed. Despaired. Running out of gas. 'We're not going to win. There's nothing we can do to win.' . . . we become depressed we don't fight anymore" (145). What the Young Man feels is "Depressed, deranged,

decapitated, dehumanized, defoliated, demented and damned"
(146). Yet he mockingly describes himself as the typical American
boy: "I am truly an American. I was made in America. Born, bred,
and raised. I have American scars on my brain. Red, white and blue. I
bleed American blood. I dream American dreams. I fuck American
girls" (148). But the American dream seems no longer viable, and he
feels himself a stranger in his own home as the band sings in "Alien
Song": "And this is the place I was born bred and raised/And it
doesn't seem like I was ever here"(149).

The Second Act

The first act of *Operation Sidewinder* was dominated by the huge
snake. As Dr. Vector had envisioned the Sidewinder as a means of ascending to a higher level, so the revolution is seen by the black conspirators as an escape and a movement upward in the process of civilization. Something has gone wrong, however; the Sidewinder has
been decapitated, and the revolution has failed, for Mickey Free has
not contaminated the reservoir. He has repented of his ways and returned to his ancient religion. The revolutionaries blame the Young
Man and hold him and Honey captive. In an effort to save the revolution they send the two out to find the Sidewinder. The second act of
the play is devoted to an effort to put the Sidewinder together again.
The emphasis now is on a spiritual rather than a political revolution,
and the renegade Indian is in the midst of the action. The Spider
Lady, an Indian sachem, relates the story of creation to the man-made
computer and stresses the deep importance of uniting its head and
tail. Humanity will then find inner peace, which will enable it to rise
above both spirit and body in a synthesis of the two. Honey and the
Young Man are joined together in an elaborate ceremony as the
Sidewinder's head and body come together again. The technology of
the Sidewinder and the ancient magic of the Spider Lady unite for a
classic *deus ex machina* ending with Honey, the Young Man, and the
Indians ascending to a higher level of existence, leaving the Technical
Desert Troops behind.

The message of *Operation Sidewinder* is basically pessimistic. Despite the spiritual growth we have seen in the Young Man, Honey,

and Mickey Free and the change in the Sidewinder from the primitive, fear-provoking snake of mythology and religion to the means of humanity's salvation, the regeneration of the American spirit does not seem possible in our society. The play foreshadows the "dropping out" of political action on the part of so many of the young—their retreat into drugs, mysticism, and the search for personal rather than societal answers.

Chapter Four
The Tooth of Crime

Leaving America

It was 1971, Shepard was twenty-eight, he had seen eighteen of his plays produced, won several Obies and foundation grants, gotten married, fathered a son, and begun to realize that he wasn't a kid anymore. He had changed, and the East Village scene was not the same as in the early 1960s. He no longer played Cowboys and Indians out in the street with Charlie Mingus, and their special camaraderie amidst all the people "who were into going to work" began to break apart. He reminisced in an interview: "Well, when I first got to New York it was wide open, you were like a kid in a fun park but then as it developed, as more and more elements came into it, things got more and more insane—you know, the difference between living in New York and working in New York became wider and wider, so that you were doing this thing called *theatre* in these little places and you were bringing your so-called experience to it, and then going back and living in this kind of tight, insular, protective way, where you were defending yourself."[1]

The defenses against the outside began to crumble. The critics had been, by and large, savage in their assessment of his first and—as it turned out to be—last uptown production, *Operation Sidewinder*. His marriage to O-Lan Johnson almost broke up over his collaboration with Patti Smith in *Cowboy Mouth*. "Also I was into a lot of drugs then—it became very difficult you know, everything seemed to be sort of shattering."[2] After the Holy Modal Rounders, an electric-fiddle group in which he played drums, disbanded, he decided to leave New York. He was not ready to go home to California, so Shepard, O-Lan, and their one-year-old son, Jesse Moyo, went to England. "I wanted to have radical change geographically and all that stuff, but I didn't want to go through a language thing."[3]

They settled in Hampstead, living off his grants and meager royalties for almost four years. Sam wrote and directed plays and tried to find out "what it means to be an American."[4] He tried to discover the origins of his art and the images from which his plays sprang: "They come from that particular part of the country, they come from that particular sort of society that you find in Southern California, where nothing is permanent, where everything could be knocked down and it wouldn't be missed, and the feel of impermanence that comes from that—that you don't belong to any sort of culture."[5] "The more distant you are from it (America), the more the implications of what you grew up with start to emerge,"[6] he told an English interviewer during his self-imposed exile. He began to pull together two themes he had been working with from the very beginning of his career into one large statement, *The Tooth of Crime*. Since his first play, *Cowboys*, he has been fascinated with the myth of the Old West and its influence on American culture. The script of this first play is now lost, but Shepard remembers why he wrote it: "Cowboys are really interesting to me—these guys, most of them really young, about sixteen or seventeen, who decided they didn't want to have anything to do with the East Coast . . . and took on that immense country, and didn't have any real rules."[7]

The Play's Themes

He developed this Western mythical theme in such other plays as *Cowboys No. 2*, *The Holy Ghostly*, *The Unseen Hand*, *Cowboy Mouth*, and *Back Dog Beast Bait*. The other theme that *The Tooth of Crime* is concerned with is the influence of rock music, which Shepard had already explored in *Melodrama Play*, *The Mad Dog Blues*, and *Cowboy Mouth*. Music has been part of Shepard's life since childhood, the only thing that he shared with a strict disciplinarian father: "He had this band . . . he was a drummer, and that's how I learned to play, just banging on his set of drums. And then I started getting better than him."[8]

The Tooth of Crime is a work that questions the very foundations of American life, that shows the inevitability of age and death, and the conflict of the son attempting to usurp the power of the father. The climax of the play is the classic shoot-out between the established top gun and the young comer. In this play, however, it is not between two gunslingers but between two rock 'n' roll stars. Shepard, when younger, always had a fantasy that he would make it in the music world. He was drawn to London in the early 1970s because he thought of it as the rock 'n' roll center of the world. In an autobiographical sketch he wrote for "News of the American Place Theatre" shortly before he left for England in 1971, he asserted, "I don't want to be a playwright. I want to be a rock 'n' roll star." In the same article he named who was important to him: "I love the Rolling Stones. I love Bridgette [*sic*] Bardot. I love Marlon Brando and James Dean and Stan Laurel and Otis Redding and Wilson Pickett and Jimmie Rodgers and Bob Dylan and The Who and Jesse James and Crazy Horse and the Big Bopper and Nina Simone and Jackson Pollock and Muhamed [*sic*] Ali and Emile Griffith and my wife O-Lan and my kid, Jesse, and Patti Smith."[9]

Very few writers have gone to the lengths that Sam Shepard has to deny any literary or intellectual influences. In his England days he told an interviewer: "I never liked books; or read very much."[10] Yet the play that he had completed shortly before the interview, *Cowboy Mouth*, is full of references to de Nerval, Villon, and Baudelaire. Later in the same interview, he mentions both Beckett and Brecht, whose influence pervades *The Tooth of Crime*, this quintessential American play. He recollects that, when still a teenager in California:

I went to this guy's house who was called a beatnick by everybody in school because he had a beard and he wore sandals. And we were listening to some jazz or something and he sort of shuffled over to me and threw a book on my lap and said, why don't you dig this, you know. I started reading this play he gave me, and it was like nothing I ever read before—it was *Waiting for Godot*. And I thought, what is this guy talking about, what is this?[11]

The Influence of Brecht

In the same interview, he pays his hommage to Brecht and to such plays as *The Rise and Fall of the City of Mahagonny* that combine music and writing. He calls Brecht his favorite playwright and mentions *Jungle of Cities* in particular. "It's a play—a bout, between these two characters, taken in a completely open-ended way, the bout is never defined as being anything but metaphysical."[12]

A more mature Shepard recalls his introduction to Brecht by both Patti Smith and Joseph Chaikin in a letter to the author. Both of them independently urged him to read Brecht. The parallels between the two writers, the young Brecht of the 1920s and the young Shepard of the 1970s, are striking:

With Brecht, I think his attraction for me, was his "tough-guy" stance in the midst of the intellectual circle of his times. His embracing aspects of the American subculture (Chicago gangsters, Alaskan opportunists, etc.). His fascination with boxing, befriending a heavyweight of the era, writing and singing songs on his guitar, his poetry, his theory, his direct involvement with actors and the problem of meeting the audience face to face with the theatrical event. His understanding of the fact of duality and that every coin has two sides. His ability to find the perfect collaboration with Kurt Weill. In other words, his voracious appetite for the life around him and his continuous adaptability to search out a true expression and put it into practice. His concern was for a total theatre but one stripped to the bare necessity.[13]

In his London interview, Shepard singled out as his favorite, *Jungle of Cities*, Brecht's third play and the first of his so-called "American" plays. To the young Germans of Brecht's generation, America was an exotic domain populated mainly by gangsters and Indians. The landscape was dominated by skyscrapers and relics of the Wild West. In the days after the First World War when *Jungle of Cities* was written, the images of America were transmitted not only by the news medium, but also by American jazz and American sports. The American dream had been familiar to the Germans from Goethe's days on and had made Walt Whitman's poetry popular. Brecht was part of one of the generations who grew up on Indian and Wild West lore. Cooper's *Leatherstocking Tales*, though long forgotten by American kids, were known as *Der Lederstrumpf* and part of every German boy's life, as were the novels of the native German Karl May, whose fanciful recreations of Indian life were the product of a prolific imagination. May, author of myriad adventure stories, had never set foot on American soil. Brecht emulated this example; he used American backgrounds in his plays only as long as he was in Europe. During his exile in California during the World War II days, he never once used an American setting.

Jungle of Cities, subtitled "Two men fighting in Chicago, the gigantic city," takes place in 1912 in the locale which remained one of Brecht's favorite settings. The story is simple. Shlink, a well-to-do middle-aged lumber merchant who is described as a Malay from Yokahama, becomes obsessed with a young clerk named Garga. He offers to buy Garga's "opinion" of a book. When the younger man indignantly refuses, a fight to the death ensues to which both men commit all their resources. Shlink uses his business, his connection to the criminal underworld, and his physical labor; while Garga's weapons become his parents, his girl friend, and his own personality. Their final duel for the possession of Garga's soul takes place on the shores of Lake Michigan. Face to face, exposed in their loneliness, Shlink commits suicide. In his preface to the play Brecht instructs the audience: "You are witnessing an inexplicable wrestling match and the destruction of a family that has come from the prairie lands to the great city jungle. In observing this battle, do not rack your brain for motives: concern yourself with the human element, evaluate the antagonists' fighting spirit impartially and concentrate your interest on the showdown" (12).[14]

Jungle of Cities has remained one of Brecht's least accessible and least performed plays. Written by a young, unrecognized artist, its expression of absolute isolation and lack of contact in an empty world seems to have preempted one of Beckett's themes. Brecht was terrified of the irrational destructive forces within him and within society, which left the individual paralyzed. Shlink and Garga appear passive throughout the play, seemingly unable to understand what drives them to ruin. Their relationship has strong sexual undertones; they are victims of a homosexual passion, doomed to a losing struggle between unconscious impulse and conscious control. The duel between the two men becomes a metaphor for the infinite loneliness of human beings and a symbol of the unspeakable coldness of human relationships. An atmosphere of icy coldness pervades the play. Their so-called wrestling match is a drama of loneliness and a struggle to reach communication, even if only by means of a battle, in a world that is

detached and defies communication.[15] The spiritual duel between
Shlink and Garga calls to mind Rimbaud's lines in: *Une Saison en
Enfer*: "Le combat spirituel est aussi brutal que le batalle d'hommes."
Rimbaud's spirit can be felt throughout the play; Garga quotes him
incessantly, and Brecht noted in his introduction that Garga resem-
bles Rimbaud in appearance. Rimbaud's scandalous relationship with
Verlaine underlines the homosexual passion between Shlink and
Garga. The young Brecht used homosexuality in several other works
of that period. It seemed to him the best expression of blind irrational
forces that do not alleviate the unbearable loneliness and the existential despair of life in an alienated urban society. Shlink expresses it:
"I've been watching animals; and love, or the warmth given off by
bodies moving in closer to each other, that is the only mercy shown to
us in the darkness. But the coupling of organs is all, it doesn't make
up for the divisions caused by speech" (83).

Jungle of Cities, which dispenses with the terminology of "acts" or
"scenes," is actually made up of ten rounds and an epilogue. As
Shepard had noted, Brecht was fascinated by boxing. In 1954 he
wrote, "It was the fierceness that interested me about this fight. And
since in those years (after 1920) I enjoyed sports, especially boxing,
one of the great mythical amusements of the giant cities beyond the
big pond—my new plays showed a fight for fighting's sake."[16] The
dehumanized abstract character of sporting events which occurred for
no other reason but for the competition alone, both fascinated Brecht
and at the same time seemed to be the metaphor for the dehumanized
world outside the arena as well as the dehumanized contestants. Yet
the fight for possession of Garga's soul seems much less a prizefight
than a chess game with human pawns. This end game makes *Jungle of
Cities* close to the concerns of our times and explains why the play has
been more popular in the last two decades than ever before. As a critic
noted in reference to a 1970 production: "Because *Jungle of Cities* not
only has tremendous dramatic impact, it also is a psychological and
intellectual power struggle between two men and in its inconsequen-
tial natural motivations anticipates Beckett and Pinter."[17]

The young Brecht who wrote *Jungle of Cities* liked to think of
himself as dispassionate and detached, attempting to repress the part

of himself that was searching desperately for warmth in a cold world. He was "looking for something to which he could be of use."[18] The words he had used to describe the protagonist of his pirate stories, Bargan, who sold out his goals, his companions, and himself for that search. In *Jungle of Cities*, Garga, the winner of the match, survived the grueling ordeal only by accepting complete isolation as the price of his freedom. It is a freedom that despite the high cost it exacts is unattainable. Garga knows "we aren't free" (35) but he wins nevertheless, for he has learned not to show any trace of feeling. He has accepted absolute isolation as the price for survival. It is a cost that Shlink is unable to pay, for he has understood that "loneliness is so powerful, there cannot even be a fight" (82). The older man loses, and Garga proclaims: "It's as simple as that, Shlink. The younger man wins" (84). Brecht has Garga end the play by not only accepting isolation, but seemingly to acclaim it: "To be alone—that's a good thing to be" (90).

Aside from the more superficial parallels between the young Brecht and Shepard—the tough-guy antiintellectualism, the fascination with the Old West and sports, popular music, be it jazz for Brecht or rock for Shepard—there are other similarities. They had both recently married and fathered a son, and they were both trying to come to terms with the ambivalent feelings of being the tough loner who survives at the cost of renouncing emotion and responsibilities, and the human being who accepts emotional ties and thus becomes vulnerable. Thus Shepard was drawn to this early Brecht play and used this metaphysical power struggle between Garga and Shlink, which can be seen as the struggle between two conflicting parts of Brecht's being, as the starting point for *The Tooth of Crime*. While the spirit of Rimbaud pervades *Jungle of Cities*, Shepard draws the title of his play from a poem by another French symbolist poet, Mallarmé:

> For vice, having gnawed by nobleness inborn
> Has marked me like you with its sterility,
> But whilst in your heart of stone there is dwelling
> A heart that the tooth of no crime can wound
> I fly, pale, undone, and by my shroud haunted
> And fearing to die if I but sleep alone.[19]

Hoss—The Hero as Rock Star

Shepard's antagonists in his duel unto death are the rock star Hoss, who fears loneliness and impending age, and the young unknown singer Crow, who takes his name and philosophy from the poems of Ted Hughes, in whose cycle of poems this ultimate nihilistic antihero of our times appears: "God went on sleeping/Crow went on laughing."[20]

Shepard recollects the writing of *The Tooth of Crime* on two separate occasions: "It started with language—it started with hearing a certain sound which is coming from the voice of this character, Hoss. And also this sort of black figure appearing on stage with this throne, and the whole kind of world that he was involved in, came from this voice. I don't mean it was any weird psychological voice in the air thing, but that it was a very real kind of sound I heard, and I started to write the play from there."[21]

That, according to the playwright, was the origin of Hoss: here is Shepard's account of the creation of the antagonist: "The character of Crow in *The Tooth of Crime* came from a yearning toward violence. A totally lethal human with no way or reason tracing how he got that way. He just appeared. He spat words that became his weapons. He doesn't 'mean' anything. He's simply following his most savage instincts. He speaks in an unheard of tongue. He needs a victim, so I gave him one. He devoured him just like he was supposed to."[22]

The framework around which Shepard builds the play is the battle of the pop charts. He creates the surrealistic science-fiction atmosphere of a world where power is decided by the media race and the weapon with which the participants battle is their style. The stage directions describe Hoss: "He enters in black leather Rocker gear with silver studs and black kid gloves. He should look like a mean Rip Torn but a little younger"(3).[23] While Hoss suggests images of Elvis Presley, Crow evokes the Rolling Stones: "He looks just like Keith Richards (co-writer with Mick Jagger of the Rolling Stones). He exudes violent arrogance and cruises the stage with true contempt."

Hoss and Crow are destined to fight for domination of their world, a battle for the music chart ratings which is defined from the beginning in violent terms. The underground terminology of the mob is used throughout. Hoss refers constantly to "his turf," his success as a "marker," of "knocking over Vegas." While the language evokes the gangster world, the situation is reminiscent of the vulnerability of the top gunslinger who is prey to every young punk who wants to make his name. Thus Shepard is consciously working with two American culture myths. Hoss and Crow are composites of the myriad influences that Shepard had been exploring all along; they are representatives of two generations of a culture based on rock, film, comics, cars, drugs, and organized crime.[24]

In his first song, "The Way Things Are," Hoss decries the passing of an era, "All the heroes are dyin' like flies," and articulates his growing doubts about his life:

> I used to believe in rhythm and blues
> Always wore my blue suede shoes.
> Now everything I do goes down in doubt. (4)

Hoss, however, is still under the illusion that he is the loner of our mythic past, that he is John Wayne, Gary Cooper, the Lone Ranger, all the heroes who, while standing alone, still represented and fought for the values of the community. He pretends to himself that he is a born killer with a lust for blood, but deep down he understands that "I'm too old-fashioned. That's it. Gotta kick out the scruples" (10).

But Hoss is a hero who has not only created himself but has been created and molded by society, has been "saved from his nature" and made into a "true genius killer," as Becky, the representative of the system, tells him. He dreams of the times when heroes made their own codes, when there was room enough in the land for a man to live freely; but without laws, without codes, ". . . it's just crime. No art involved. No technique, no finesse," says Hoss (24).

Hoss is approaching middle age, and he fears growing obsolete in a society that discards the artist when a new fad comes along. He fears that it is all slipping away before he has had a chance to grasp it: "I feel so trapped. So fucking unsure. Everything's a mystery. I had it all in the palm of my hand. The gold. The silver. I knew. I was sure. How could it slip away like that?"(38).

Hoss is beginning to question the foundations of his life; he wants something more out of life, something that his astrologer defines as "something durable, something lasting"(8), in a society that is getting more and more rootless and devoid of lasting values. With fame has come alienation. Hoss laments: "We don't have the whole picture. . . . We're insulated from what's happening by our own fame"(10). With alienation, comes doubt, "I don't trust the race no more" (10). Doubt is a poor weapon against the hungry gypsies who live outside the pale, who are not burdened with rules. Hoss is aware of the vulnerability of an older order, and the inevitability of being replaced, "That's how we started, ain't it?" (17).

While Hoss tries to delude himself that he is a born killer with a lust for blood, he knows he has become dependent on a complicated bureaucratic back-up system that has dulled his instinct for survival. He even needs interpreters for his moon chart. While he rails against the restrictions of the system, he has accepted it, and he cannot break away from it. He has become a domesticated animal, perhaps longing for the wild but no longer able to survive in it. "Look at me now. Impotent. Can't strike a kill unless the charts are right" (36).

Hoss still talks of "moving by the sixth sense," of "smelling blood," but when he realizes that his turf has been invaded, he falls back upon the law. "It's against the code," he complains. Hoss understands that no matter what he may pretend, he cannot go back to an earlier stage of development, for his style is geared to be played against an ordered, regulated background of society. He has become hooked on security, on law and order, and he would be "ripped up in a night" (29) in the jungle outside the code.

Hoss, who had always thought of himself as the young conquerer, has to face the reality that there are always young gypsies on the way up, but "It's funny finding myself on the other side" (26). Hoss is speaking for Sam Shepard, the young iconoclast, approaching thirty in an age where the slogan is "never trust anyone over thirty."

Hoss envies the young gypsies their freedom from the rules and the system and bemoans the price he has had to pay for security: "We ain't free no more, Goddamit. We ain't flying in the eye of contempt. We've become respectable and safe. Soft, mushy, chewable ass-lickers" (22). But the system is no longer viable. The gypsies are exerting an ever-greater force, and even Becky, who had taught Hoss the code, urges survival tactics now. "Temporary suspension" of the code, she counsels (20). But Hoss understands that the end is near: "I think the whole system's gettin' shot to shit. I think the code's going down the tubes. These are gonna be the last days of honor"(26). Trying to find some sense in his life, he regrets the lack of authenticity in it. "Everything just happened. Just fell like cards. I never made a decision"(27). Not only does Hoss see his life lacking a purpose, but he sees dangers to the self: "You'd be O.K., Becky, if you had a self. So would I. Something to fall back on in a moment of doubt or terror or even surprise" (37).

Hoss begins to understand that while he, along with everyone else, was compulsively pursuing the top of the charts, the country, the dream has disappeared: "What about the country? Ain't there any farmers left? Ranchers, cowboys, open space? Nobody just living their life?" (29). The freedom that Becky had promised him for playing the game, does not exist: "What free? How free? I'm tearin' myself inside out from this fuckin' sport. That's free? That's being alive? I just wanna have some fun. I wanna be a fuck-off again. I don't wanna compete no more" (29). Hoss, like Shepard, is longing for the days of youth, of irresponsibility, knowing that they will never return.

The futility of the inevitable duel with the gypsy killer becomes clearer and clearer to Hoss, and so is the only meaningful action left to him: "Suicide, man. Maybe Little Willard was right. Blow your fuckin' brains out. The whole thing is a joke. He's my brother and I gotta kill him. Jimmy Dean was right. Drive the fuckin' Spider till it stings you to death. Crack up your soul, Jackson Pollock! Duane Allman" (36). And so, realizing his ultimate loneliness, "Alone. That's me. Alone. That's us. All fucking alone. All of us," Hoss meets his adversary (37).

The Antihero—Crow

Crow is cool, guiltless, violent; he is the image of the survivor who made it because he is completely antisocial, who has "called the bluff in God's own face" (26). Unlike Hoss, he can make it without fantasy, without "illusion to add toward confusion" (4). He is rootless, restless, and completely without feeling. Crow seems to be a new species of mankind, a creature out of a science-fiction nightmare, an evolutionary development that goes beyond emotion and is protean in its ability to adapt. Shepard shows the interaction between man as we have known him (Hoss) and man of the future (Crow). Hoss, strung out, afraid, and defensive, is very human. He still holds onto tradition and history. Crow is no longer involved with anything; he is cold, icy and alone, and is beyond the search for meaning—in the duel and in life. Crow does not look for or need an authentic style; he adapts whichever one suits his purpose. He is not only past the emotional level, but the creative one as well. Crow is the consummate epigone. Hoss tells him: "You're a master adapter. A visionary adapter" (73). While Hoss is still trying to find an authentic artistic expression, "I'm pulled and pushed around from one image to another. Nothing takes solid form. Nothin' sure and final. Where do I stand?" Crow answers him, "Alone" (65). Hoss makes a last-ditch attempt at survival, but he knows that he can never follow Crow's suggestion to "Get mean. There's too much empathy. There's too much pity" (66). Like Shlink, Hoss knows that being "Mean, and tough and cool. Untouchable. A true killer," was not his style. He cries out, "It ain't me. It ain't me" (71). He has lost a duel whose ground rules he no longer understands, and he chooses the one authentic choice that is left to him—death: "I couldn't take my life in my hands while I was alive but now I can take it in death. I'm a born marker, Crow Bait. That's more than you'll ever be. Now stand back and watch some true style. The mark of a lifetime. A true gesture that won't never cheat on itself 'cause it's the last of its kind. It can't be taught or copied or stolen or sold. It's mine. An original. It's my life and my death in one clean shot" (74).

The Duel

The duel is one of style, of words. Hoss chooses it over one using weapons or machines, as a last means of conquering the feeling of isolation and alienation. But like Shlink, he learns that our loneliness is so deep that we cannot even touch each other in battle. It becomes a war fought with the weapons of language. Hoss's language is drawn from all our American pop culture heroes—from cowboys to race track touts, from gangsters to rock musicians. It embodies the shifting identity of our cultural heroes. Crow's language is weird, part science fiction, part computer—a humanoid language that defies communication.

The first round is Crow's all the way. It is full of sadomasochistic, homoerotic images, evoking Shlink's words that not even sexual contact can bridge our isolation. The second round seems to be going to Hoss as he berates Crow for not knowing the roots and origins of his music. Hoss is using the idiom of the black jazz and blues musicians and accuses Crow of wanting "a free ride on a black man's back" (59). Even though he shakes Crow somewhat, the referee calls the round a draw, showing that history and tradition are no longer relevant in the new order that Crow symbolizes.

The third round is short as Crow moves in for the kill, mocking Hoss's inability to change styles as the moment calls for, his obsolescence in a world ruled by Crow. Hoss loses because he is human and thus vulnerable. Crow's only style is power and survival, unburdened by the need for identity, security, or human contact. If Garga learns how to survive this way, Crow *is* this way; he *is* power.

As Shlink and Garga showed Brecht's ambivalent attitudes at the time he wrote *Jungle of Cities*, so Crow and Hoss act out conflicting emotions within Shepard. The play, however, leaves little doubt in the viewer's mind that the writer's ultimate sympathy lies with Hoss. Shepard is warning that our society seems doomed to create only Crows. In a very Brechtian way Shepard suggests to the audience that if the world as we know it is to survive, society had better be changed so that the essentially American hero and his values can survive.

Brecht not only influenced the structure of *The Tooth of Crime*, but his theories of the drama pervade the play. In an interview Shepard gave during his stay in England, he said; "I wanted the music in *The Tooth of Crime* so that you could step out of the play for a minute, every time a song comes, and be brought to an emotional comment on what's been taking place in the play."[25] This is, of course, what Brecht used his songs for—as a means of distancing, of estrangement. The songs in *The Tooth of Crime* do exactly that, from Hoss's first "The Way Things Are," to Crow's final statement, "Rollin' Down," they not only underline the action on stage, but focus the audience's attention on the importance of what they've just seen.

Becky's first song, "Nasty Times," sounds the theme of loneliness and isolation, "I just like to lay back on my own" (59). Toward the end of the play when Crow tries to explain to Hoss "pure focus" (69) an absolutely neutral emotional plane from which he operates, Becky acts out an autoseduction scene. Human isolation is so absolute that even sex is possible only on an onanistic level. It is the ultimate portrayal of aloneness.

The language Shepard uses in this play is a composite of a number of cants and argots. It seemed strange enough to prompt a Chicago critic to print a glossary of Shepard's language in *The Tooth of Crime*. She pointed out to the potential players that they would have to understand that the Killers Shepard refers to are "metaphoric to connect the cold brutality of a crime machine with the working of the rock industry," and that a "Gestalt Match figure" was a talking duel.[26] The most intriguing word that Shepard uses in the play, "to suss," meaning to find out, seems to have been made up by him. Shepard's use of language serves not only to delineate the differences between the protagonists, but to underline the shifting identity of the American hero from cowboy to gangster to rock star.

As in many of Shepard's plays, we are in a world of men where women such as Becky act out male sexual fantasies. She is seen at first as the voice of the establishment that has kept Hoss toeing the line, the eternal woman who forces men to conform, but switches points of view in the middle of the play and then urges Hoss to relinquish the identity he has created for himself. At the end of the play she becomes part of Crow's retinue as part of the spoils of battle. An interesting contrast to Becky is provided by the buddy figure, Cheyenne, the typical cowboy sidekick, who remains true to Hoss and his values and refuses to adopt Crow's style.

In *The Tooth of Crime* Shepard has created a truly original play which integrates the influence of two great Europeans—Brecht and Beckett—into a truly American idiom. If Garga was a German translation from the French into an American, then Hoss is the truly American hero who is not a translation but an original. The Americanization of these essentially European traditions is important to Shepard. Commenting on the Theater of the Absurd in particular, he writes that it "was a movement that more or less coincided with Off-Broadway but it remained European in its psychological stance. I felt it was important that an American playwright speak with an American tongue, not only in a vernacular sense, but that he should inhabit the stage with American being. The American playwright should snarl and spit, not whimper and whine."[27]

Chapter Five

The Way Home

Action

Despite Shepard's passionate avowal of the need for a distinctly American theatrical stance, *Action*, the one-act play he wrote during the end of his London stay, is very close to the European Theater of the Absurd. The play, whose plot negates the title, is a quartet for four noncommunicating voices. They are looking for a mechanism of sorts with which to fill the void in which they live and for their own identities and personalities which they invent for themselves. "You act yourself out," says Shooter (133).[1] The four of them search for some activity to take their minds off the terror and boredom of their lives. The setting, the references, and the images in *Action* are recognizably American. The picture of America shown is one of disorientation. The characters cannot find their place in society any more that they can find their place in the book they are reading throughout the play. The two women, Lupe and Liza, shown in completely stereotyped roles, seem less lost as they go about cooking, cleaning, and performing other "women's work." Shooter and Jeep are completely adrift in a confusing world in which they search for some direction, some reason to take action. The play projects an overwhelming feeling of being trapped, of being in a world where there is no exit. The situation that Jeep describes recalls the famous Marcel Marceau routine of the man building an invisible prison whose walls shrink around him, crushing him: "I'd have this dream come to me that the walls were moving in. It was like a sweeping kind of terror that struck me. Then something in me would panic. I wouldn't make a move. I'd just be standing there very still, but inside something would leap like it was trying to escape. And then the leap would come up against something. It was like an absolutely helpless leap there was no possibility of escape"(145).

Shepard still considers *Action* to be "without doubt a major break-through for me. I wrote it in three days sitting at a baroque black mahogany desk. It belonged to an Indian landlady who was storing it as an antique and it had dragons carved into the legs. . . ."[2]

Action is the most humorless of Shepard's plays and the one that in the parlance of his characters is unrelievedly "heavy." It continues to be presented on double bills with, for instance, one-acters by Ionesco, thus cementing it even closer to the Theater of the Absurd, despite its author's protest. The feeling of isolation the play projects is no doubt partially due to Shepard's experiences of surviving apart from the America in which he is so deeply rooted.

Geography of a Horse Dreamer

Geography of a Horse Dreamer was the first of Shepard's plays that he directed. He has since become more and more involved in the whole process of theater and has become more and more of a "Theatermensch." His involvement with directing came about mainly through his dissatisfaction with what other directors had done with his work. He was particularly angry at Richard Schechner's New York production of *Tooth of Crime*, which he felt distorted the play:

[Schechner] wants to experiment with the environment of the theatre, which is Okay. I've nothing against it. Except when you write a play it sets up certain assumptions about the context in which it's to be performed; and in that play they had nothing to do with what Schechner sets up in the theatre—I'd rather that the experimentation took place with something that left itself open to that—a play that from the start defines its context as undefinable, so that you can fuck around with it if you want to.[3]

In a letter to Schechner, in which he accuses him of an unsympathetic reading of the play, Shepard voices a complaint echoed by playwrights since time immemorial: "It seems to me that the reason someone wants to put a play together in a production is because they are pulled to its vision. If that's true then it seems they should respect the form the vision takes place in and not merely extrapolate the language and invent another form which isn't the play."[4]

In *Geography of a Horse Dreamer*, Shepard once again expressed his overwhelming concern for the fate of the artist exploited by society. His hero is a young man gifted with the ability to "dream winners," who is held prisoner by a group of gangsters and forced to use his talent for their gain. His genius fades under these conditions, and he begins to dream dog winners. He is close to madness when he is rescued by two cowboys. The language Shepard explores here is that of the classic American mystery writers of the 1930s: "I was using language from Raymond Chandler, from Dashiell Hammett—from the 'thirties, which to me is a beautiful kind of language, and very idiomatic of a period in which America was really strong."[5]

Shepard had been living in London for over three years when he directed *Geography of a Horse Dreamer*. Always extremely sensitive to language, he began to notice "subtle changes in the rhythm and construction" of his speech: "In order to accommodate these new configurations in the way a sentence would overblow itself (as is the English tendency), I found myself adding English characters to my plays. *Geography* was written in London, and there's only one truly American character in the play."[6]

Shepard, who had loved horse racing during his adolescence in California, was beginning to like the English working-class sport of dog racing. In fact, he raced two greyhounds at the track in Walthamstow and Birmingham. Expressed clearly in *Geography of a Horse Dreamer* is the writer's fear of becoming alienated from his roots, the fears of beginning to dream dog winners instead of horse winners. If there was any rescue from the gangsters who held the artist prisoner, who caused his vision to dim, it would have to come from America's past, from its cultural heritage—the cowboys. It was time to go home, really home. And so toward the end of 1974, Sam Shepard took his family home to California, to San Francisco. Before Shepard settled down (he later avoided leaving California at any cost), he said goodbye to his traveling days in a unique and symbolic way. He accompanied Bob Dylan on a tour of the Rolling Thunder Revue in order to write a screenplay for a film about the Revue. The movie was doomed by "a combination of technical and psychological screw ups,"[7] which Shepard chronicled in *Rolling Thunder Logbook*.

Angel City

Sam Shepard's images and visions have always been deeply influenced by film, so it seems entirely appropriate that he explore "his
own cinematic imagination and his impulse toward a filmic vocabu-
lary."[8] His theme in *Angel City* is once again power, here played
against the background of movies and their compelling hold on our
imaginations and lives. It shows equally their allure, their promise to
bring meaning into drab lives, and the destructive danger that living
in dream machines bring to the individual viewer, the artist, and
society. Like Rabbit, the script doctor, Shepard had had some unfor-
tunate experience with movies even before the Rolling Thunder
Revue disaster. Antonioni had hired him to work on the script of
Zabriskie Point in the mid-1960s. He had chosen him, according to
Shepard's recollections in a *Village Voice* interview, because: "I had a
play called *Icarus's Mother* which had an airplane in it, he figured that
since he had an airplane in his movie we had something in common."[9]

Unlike Rabbit in *Angel City*, who learns the business so well that he
becomes the ultimate purveyor of the "green slime," Shepard pulled
out: "I didn't know how to continue with what Antonioni wanted.
He wanted political repartee and I just didn't know how. Plus I was
24 and just wasted by the experience. It was like a nightmare. I was
surrounded by MGM and all that stuff—to submerge yourself in that
world of limousines and hotels and rehashing and pleasing Carlo
Ponti is just: I spent almost two years off and on around the whole
business."[10]

The green slime in *Angel City* that oozes over the stage at the end of
the play is the standard horror movie material that becomes the
metaphor of the pervading influence of the movies on our life and our
imagination. The alienating effect that film can have on our perception of reality is expressed by Scoons, the secretary who, according to
stage directions, speaks in "a kind of flattened monotone, almost as if
another voice is speaking through her," "I look at the screen and I
am the screen. I'm not me. I don't know who I am. I look at the movie
and I am the movie. I am the star. I am the star in the movie. For days
I am the star and I'm not me. I'm me being the star. I look at my life

when I come down. I look and I hate my life when I come down. I hate my life not being a movie . . ."(21).

Tympani, the drummer in *Angel City*, is looking for "the rhythm . . . the one special rhythm which will drive men crazy" (22). The hypnotic rhythm he finally finds transports him into oblivion along with those who like Miss Scoons succumb to it. The artist is no more immune to the seductive dreams and images he spins than are the entranced spectators.

Suicide in B Flat

Sam Shepard continued to explore the world of the creative artist in *Suicide in B Flat*,[11] a play in which he changes musical styles. Many of his plays have been strongly aligned with music, to the rock 'n' roll and Country Western idiom. Here the music played is jazz, and the improvisations are subtle and complex. The "plot" of *Suicide in B Flat*, if it can be called one, involves the investigation of the murder (or was it?) of a jazzman by two Raymond Chandler—type detectives. But who, indeed, did shoot the piano player? Or is he in fact dead at all? Can one, as the play asks, kill a myth? In an abstract way, Shepard plays with the collision of myths and reality within an artist and within a society.

The play abounds with some of Shepard's most dazzling vocal fireworks as he delves into the sources of his own creativity and the price the artist must inevitably pay for the act of creation. He describes the musician's first encounter with sound and his intoxication with it: "Music as an extension of sound. An organization. Another way of putting it. He's disappointed. He's disappointed and exhilarated at the same time. Exhilarated because he sees an opening. An adventure. A way inside" (122).[12] But the way inside is threatening to the personality of the artist: "He's driven toward it in a way most men consider dangerous and suicidal. His production is abundant. Non-stop. Endlessly winding through unheard-of-before symphonies. Concertos beyond belief"(123). The rush of creativity threatens to overwhelm him and he becomes: "A victim of circumstances beyond his control. His music was driving him mad. He began to feel certain he was possessed. Not as if by magic but by his own gift. His own voracious hunger for sound became like a demon"(129).

The alleged victim, Niles, appears, wondering, "What if it turns out to be harder playing dead than it was playing alive?"(136). The musician tells of his childhood: "I lived in a tin house with a corrugated roof that sounded like Balinese cymbals when it rained. It rained tropical rains there. The kind that sound like they'll never end. And you'll be washed away. And at night the laundry flaps. The sheets snap like wet whips. They're all tied down by ropes so that the Japanese won't steal them. And your mother has a .45 Automatic Colt revolver with an extra clip in her pocket book just in case"(136). In recollections of his own childhood, Shepard recalls: "I remember the tin-roofed huts that we lived in, because it used to rain a lot, and the rain would make this incredible sound on the tin roof. Also there were a lot of Japanese on the island, who had been forced back into living in the caves, and they would come down and steal clothes off the clothes-lines, and food and stuff. All the women were issued army Lugers, and I remember my mother shooting at them."[13]

The playwright and his character are in the words that Shepard has Niles say at the end of the play, "so exactly like you that we're exactly the same"(153). Like Niles, who tries to rid himself of the identity myths and role models that he fears have cramped his artistic style, so Shepard has expressed from time to time a similar desire: "to try a whole different way of writing now, which is very stark and not so flashy and not full of mythic figures."[14]

Curse of the Starving Class

1976 was an enormously productive year for Sam Shepard. In addition to *Suicide in B Flat*, which was produced by the Yale Repertory Theatre, and *Angel City*, which was done at San Francisco's Magic Theatre, Joseph Papp produced *Curse of the Starving Class* at the New York Shakespeare Festival. It won Shepard the Obie, awarded by the *Village Voice* to Off Broadway work, for the best new American Play for the 1976/77 season, the highest honor yet awarded him. In the words of Ross Wetzstein, "Sam Shepard finally wrote the important play everyone had been waiting for."[15] *Curse of the Starving Class* is Shepard's first in-depth exploration of the decline and fall of the American family, a subject he had first touched upon in *Rock Garden* and which he was to conclude definitively in *Buried Child*.

"What kind of a family is this?" asks Emma at the beginning of the play.[16] It is a family that is crumbling and threatened. It cannot withstand the destructive forces crushing it from without and the disintegration from within. The central image of the play is hunger, a metaphor with which Shepard has worked before and is to again in *Buried Child* and *Tongues*. The spiritual starvation destroys the family, despite the efforts of the son to hold it together. The faith the family has in not belonging to the starving class is shattered. The spiritual starvation of America is so pervasive that none can escape. "I can feel this country close like it was part of my bones," says Wesley, the son, who in vain tries to stave off the impending ruin (59). But, Shepard is saying in this play, it is too late to save the land which has nourished us. In a Chekhovian vision Wesley sees: "There'll be bulldozers crashing through the orchard. There'll be giant steel balls crashing through the walls. There'll be foremen with their sleeves rolled up and blue prints under their arms. There'll be steel girders spanning acres of land. Cement pilings. Pre-fab walls. Zombie architecture, owned by invisible Zombies, built by Zombies for the use and convenience of other Zombies"(83). As Wesley prophetically says: "It means more than losing a house. It means losing a country"(83).

The family, that metaphor for society, is no longer viable in *Curse of the Starving Class*. The father is an irresponsible drunk. The mother has repressed whatever feeling she ever had for her children, and only wants to get out. The children are cheated and stunted by lack of love—the ultimate starvation. Their fierce resentment of society that has substituted dreams of affluence for the reality of family warmth is symbolized by Emma's wild horseback ride which culminates in the shooting up of a road house. How unnourishing the American family has become is vividly underlined for the audience by the mountain of artichokes which litter the stage. The refrigerator is filled only with these unnourishing vegetables.

The word "curse" in the title refers to the inevitability of generation after generation repeating the same meaningless acts. The curse of the father is passed on to the son. As Weston, the father, says: "I never saw my old man's poison until I was much older than you. Much older. And then you know how I recognized it?—Because I saw myself infected with it"(87). Wesley, the son, finally seeing the impossibility of averting the curse, puts on Weston's filthy old clothes: "I could feel him coming in and me going out. Just like the change of the guards"(113).

The "curse" also refers to menstruation, a physical state that is amply commented upon in the play. If the "poison" Weston refers to is transmitted from father to son, then the "curse" is transmitted from mother to daughter. But Shepard's pessimistic view of the world leads him to overlook the fact that this female "curse" is indeed a misnomer. It is not a symbol of death, but one of life, one of fertility and procreation. Perhaps if American society were less intent on carrying out the eternal power struggle between father and son, which will continue to "poison"' life and were to view the "curse" as a blessing, a more nutrient way of life could flourish.

Seduced

In the figure of Howard Hughes, the man who "dreamed himself into another shape," who "made himself up"(114),[17] and the myths surrounding him, Shepard found a perfect symbol of his vision of America. Hughes, or Henry Hackamore, as he is called in *Seduced*, is a man consumed by power, the ultimate perversion of the individualistic American hero. Hackamore is a demented paranoid crazy, "his hair is shoulder length and white, long white beard, long cork-screw shaped fingernails and toe nails"(71). The industrial empire he built with its pyramiding of wealth and power is devoid of any feeling or humanity. Hackamore was seduced by the American dream of power and success which turned into the madness of the drive for power which is directed toward death rather than life and sanity. Shepard's vision of America in this play is so bleak that it might better have been called "Raped" rather than *Seduced*. The imagery and language are full of violence and of the sense of having been violated. Here is Shepard's vision of America:

My vision? That's right. My vision. I still see. Even in the dark, I still see.
Do you want to know what I see, Raul? It's the same thing I've always seen. I
saw myself. Alone. Standing in open country. Flat, barren. Wasted. As far as
the eyes could take in. Enormous country. Primitive. Screaming with
hostility toward men. Toward us. Toward me. As though men didn't belong
here. As though men were a joke in the face of it. I heard rattlesnakes
laughing. Coyotes. Cactus stabbing the blue air. Miles of heat and wind and
red rock where nothing grew but the sand. And far off, invisible little men
were huddled against it in cities. In tiny towns. In organizations. Protected.
I saw the whole world of men as pathetic. Sad, demented little morons
moving in circles. Always in the same circles. Always away from the truth.
Getting smaller and smaller until they finally disappear.(111)

Rape similes abound in *Seduced*. Hackamore has created an airless,
lifeless space around himself. When he feels a human presence he calls
out: "We've been penetrated. They've found their way in!"(84). The
women he has flown into this womblike space he has fashioned are two
macho fantasies of sex goddesses: "One time or another I've penetrated every single one of them—right to the core. Straight to the
heart"(81). He has cut himself off completely from any kind of feeling
and human contact. "Nothing from outside touches me"(90), he
explains to Luna. "It's by mutual arrangement. I don't touch it, it
doesn't touch me. That's what happens when you rape something,
isn't it? . . . After that you don't touch. There's a repulsion between
both sides"(91). Hackamore has been "raped" by the dream that
America can no longer fulfill and, in turn, has raped the promise of
the country by his demented craving for a "fool-proof organization"(81) at the cost of humanity. In stereotyped, exaggerated macho
terms, Hughes/Hackamore pays tribute to the life force which he sees
inherent in the female. It is an "awesome" power which, however, he
has violated and "penetrated" in order to make it subservient to him.
He can see relationships only in terms of violation and conquest: "It's
a force. With men I was always a master. They'd lick my heels. Men
become dogs in a second. It is the female that's dangerous. Uncontrol-
lable. Cat-like"(92).

He sees women always as objects, as means to an end: "I needed
women! Women more than anything. Women to fill me up! To ease

me into the other world. To see me across. To bring me ecstacy and salvation"(93).

But Luna and Miami are unable to keep him from falling, as he begs them to. They are only dream figures, as the stage directions read: "They've stepped directly out of Henry's past without aging" (93). At the end of the play, betrayed by his buddy and servant Raul, Henry understands that he has been raped and seduced by the American dream: "I was taken by the dream and all the time I thought I was taking it. It was a sudden seduction. Abrupt. Almost like rape. You could call it rape. I gave myself up. Sold it all down the river"(114).

The demented Hackamore, dressed in his flying regalia, stands on his bed and spreads out his arms: "I'm the demon they invented. Everything they aspired to. The nightmare of the nation! It's me, Raul. Only me!"(116). Like Frankenstein's monster, Henry seems to be indestructible now. He withstands Raul's bullets, chanting: "I'm dead to the world but I've never been born"(116). He has become the perfect symbol of sterility and destruction who even denies having been born of woman—for he has been invented without benefit of humans or humanity.

Inacoma

In 1977 Shepard had time to explore his interest in the ongoing relationship among actors, directors and writers which he had begun investigating in England when he first began directing his own work. At that time he formed a liason with the Magic Theatre, which had been the first to produce one of his plays in his native California (*La Turista*, in 1970). The company, under the direction of John Lion, had also done the West Coast premiere of *Action* and the world premiere of *Angel City*. Armed with a $15,000 Rockefeller grant, Shepard, together with eight actors and eight musicians, collaboratively developed an improvisational play called *Inacoma*. The play is based on the hallucinations, fantasies, and altered states of consciousness experienced by a patient in a coma: "All I could visualize was a hospital bed, the coma victim and creature-characters. Then various scenes would start popping up, all out of context and wandering in and out of different realities. The scenes were joined by sounds of breathing, the music, then back to sounds. I kept abandoning the idea of even starting to write something because the subject became too vast and uncontrollable."[18]

The play that developed out of the workshop's collaborative process was never more than a work-in-process that permitted Shepard to return to a mode of creating that he had first tried with *Forensic and the Navigators* at the Theatre Genesis. He had also worked with Joseph Chaikin at the Open Theatre in the production of *Terminal* and *Nightwalk*, an association that he was to pick up later in his career.

Chapter Six
Buried Child
The Theme Restated

One of Shepard's recurring themes is the decay of the American family, which can readily be seen as a synonym for the nonviability of today's American society. The playwright sounded this theme very early in his career in the one-act play *Rock Garden*, which he still considers among the best of his one-act plays. He treats the theme more fully in *Curse of the Starving Class*, which marks the next stage of development that culminates in Shepard's definitive treatment of the American family in *Buried Child*. The family plays are among the few of Shepard's works that dispense with music. *Buried Child*, the play that brought him the 1979 Pulitzer Prize for drama, is mockingly described by its author as a "typical Pulitzer Prize winning play." While he denies having written the play for that purpose, he nevertheless admits that, "If I was gonna write a play that would win the Pulitzer Prize, I think it would have been that play."[1] Couching the problems of America in the metaphor of the breakdown of the American family, *Buried Child* makes them more accessible and understandable to the audience. It brought this "epitaph for the American family as an institution"[2] an Off Broadway run that was a record for a Shepard play. It was a work that could have easily been moved to Broadway and, bolstered by the publicity connected to the prize, have had a respectable number of performances. Shepard, however, balked at this:

. . . my reservations about Broadway go beyond the "Commercialism" stigma. I really believe the theatre experience is an experience of intimacy, a personal transaction between actors and audience. As the audience increases in size, the intimacy is reduced and becomes absorbed in a kind of mass psychology. Reactions sweep through the audience overtaking the individual and causing him to believe they're his own reactions. Sometimes this sensation may even be thrilling but it often has little to do with, and even robs the person of his own response.[3]

Buried Child, like the majority of Shepard's plays, takes place in the most ordinary of backgrounds, a shabby rural living room. Here Shepard sets out to expose not Pinter's "weasel under the cocktail table" but the child buried in the backyard—the decaying corpse of the American dream. The atmosphere in the family is stifling, repressive, sterile, and noncaring, for the essential element of love is missing. The action is played against a background of archaic, primeval power struggles. It portrays a savage world expressing exclusive patriarchal values of violence and dominance.

The American dream of bountiful Eden, the poetic image of the land, seems no longer fulfillable in an industrial, mechanized, computerized, and dehumanizing society. Shepard suggests the possibility of returning to an America that was once strong, held promises, and nourished its people. This return, however, is possible only when America's reality is confronted without the veil of Norman Rockwell sentimentality, when the crimes of the past are acknowledged and atoned for, and the young can be enlisted to accept their responsibility for the recreation of the dream. From that point of *Buried Child* is the perfect post-Vietnam play, which exhorts the young to turn away from the drop-out world of drugs and cults and the narcissistic concern with "me."

The Mythic World

Shepard has always been noted for his propensity for mythmaking. The myths he utilized in *Buried Child* go far back into archaic times to give substance to the struggle of the father to keep his son from gaining power. Dodge, the father who has always "dodged" responsibility for his sons, is the archetypal threatening father whose infanticidal impulse still haunts man's subconscious. The love-denying father ("You think just because people propagate they have to love their offsprings") projects his violence to the mother: "You never saw a bitch eat her puppies?"(54).[4]

The only paternal attribute that Dodge exults in is the macho one of potency: "You know how many kids I've spawned?"(55). But even Dodge senses that this kind of procreation is death rather than life oriented, a murder of the once fecund American tradition. "There's not a living soul behind me. Not a one"(55). He fears his sons, for the prophecy cannot be denied, fate cannot be averted. As Cronus feared death at the hands of his progeny, as Laius tried to escape the prophesied meeting with Oedipus at the crossroad, Dodge is terrified of losing control: "They'll steal your bottle! They'll cut your hair! They'll murder your children"(38).

Ironically, the sons of Dodge are portrayed as impotent against him, and the only children who have been murdered have been killed by him alone. Dodge's three sons are a mockery. Tilden is described as "profoundly burned out and displaced"(16), a walking wounded terribly injured in battle, yet carrying within him memories of a once fruitful land. He is a man whose troubles are explained as: "He got mixed up"(55). Tilden's belief in the fertile paradise that once was and can be again is constantly concretized before the audiences's eyes by the seemingly never ending supplies of corn and carrots that are dumped on stage by him.

Bradley, the second son, is the personification of the ultimate male castration fear. He has a wooden leg that is taken from him by Shelly and Vince, making his helplessness a symbol of impotence. In his hands he carries the instrument of his castration, the scissors with which he threatens and terrorizes Dodge. The impotent son is unable to replace his father; able only to make the father as impotent as he is by cutting off his hair. Dodge, like a modern-day Samson, has lost his power and potency to the now castrating figure of the son. Bradley, who mocks Tilden, and Vince, who ultimately mocks Bradley, are acting out the primeval, brutal Cain and Abel conflict of brotherhood. The castrated, crippled Bradley has all the cruelty of the deeply threatened and all the self-delusion of the powerless: "There was a time, when I had to take that tone of voice from pretty near everyone. Him for one! Him and that half-brain that just ran outa here. They don't talk to me like that now"(50). Bradley deceives himself that he has power, but his words are belied by his action on stage. His sterility is shown by the ultimate act of violent and cruel powerlessness—his fellatio rape of Shelly at the end of the second act.

The third son, Ansel, has been dead for years before the play begins. Halie, the mother, fantasizes him into an avenging hero. "He would have seen we were repaid"(20). The irony is obvious. What should he have repaid his parents for? What do you repay a family that mutilates and kills its offspring?

Into this claustrophobic family enter the two outsiders, Vince (the conqueror) and Shelly. Vince is the archetypal questing hero searching for "his heritage." Vince, the son without a mother, is impelled to carry out his destiny. "Vince has this thing about his family now," says Shelly (32). He is the personification of the unconscious male womb creation myth, doomed forever to search for the unknowable mother. Neither Dodge nor Tilden acknowledges Vince. To his plea, "I'm their son," Dodge answers, "You're no son of mine. I've had sons in my time and you're not one of them"(42).

"Have I committed an unpardonable offense?" Vince cries out (41). Tilden, his supposed father, recognizes only a glimpse of him: "I thought I recognized something about him—I thought I saw a face inside the face"(44). Was that face the face of innocence betrayed? The face of an American eager for adventure, for the fulfillment of the dream, the face of the child before it was killed?

The crime of which Vince is guilty is his denial of the caring and nurturing tradition in favor of the violent tradition personified by Dodge. He is Dodge's true son. His long monologue at the end of the third act, his "aria" (Shepard becomes operatic at times) describing his meeting with his daemon, clarifies this:

I could see myself in the windshield. My face. My eyes. I studied everything about it. As though I was looking at another man. As though I could see his whole face behind him. Like a mummy's face. I saw him dead and alive at the same time. In the same breath. . . . And then his face changed. His face became his father's face. Same bones. Same eyes . . . and his father changed to his grandfather's face. And it went on like that. Changing. Clear on back to faces I'd never seen before but still recognized. . . . (70)

The Betrayal of the Dream

The alienation that the betrayal of the American dream brings is shown by changing Vince's speech from the first to the third person in the middle of the monologue. Vince will never be able to make the earth and the dream fruitful again, for he has accepted the world of power, domination, and violence. This son, cut off forever from the world of the mother, has been fated to usurp the equally sterile reign of Dodge. When Vince reenters the stage in the third act in a drunken rage, breaking empty bottles, he orchestrates his alliance to the violent world of Dodge by the singing of the Marine Hymn. Dodge understands that Vince will replace him. "Maybe I should come in and usurp your territory," Vince announces (67). Dodge accedes to him. "The house goes to my Grandson Vince"(69). Vince, however, is death, not life, directed. While expounding his plans for making the farm fruitful again, he continues to torture Bradley. When Bradley finally crawls off stage, Vince pulls the blanket away from him and throws it around his own shoulders, just as Bradley had taken the same blanket from Dodge. It shows an endless progression from one violent man to another, dooming us to sterility and death. When the minister suggests that Vince go to Halie and comfort her, he only answers: "My grandmother? There's no one else in the house"(76). It was his last chance to act humanely and humanly. That chance refused, Vince lies down on the couch in the same position we saw Dodge in at the play's opening. The stage direction reads, "His body is in the same relationship to Dodge's"(72), who lies dead on the stage covered with Halie's roses "that almost cover up the stench of sin" (58).

Only one character consistently believes in the land's fruitfulness, Tilden (the tiller of the soil), who appears in the play as the fool purified by suffering. He is the only one who does not try to repress the sins that have been committed and sees the vegetables growing in the backyard that has lain fallow for years. Dodge had planted the corn, but he can neither see nor harvest it. He failed to give it nurturance as he failed to nuture his sons. He never responded to their needs as Tilden plaintively says, "You shoulda worried about me then . . . I was lonely"(19).

Even to Tilden the sudden fecundity of the earth is puzzling. "It's a mystery to me," he says (23). The only one who can see what Tilden sees is Halie at the end of the play: "Tilden was right about the corn you know. I've never seen such corn. Have you taken a look at it lately? Tall as a man already. This early in the year. Carrots too. Potatoes. Peas. It's like a paradise out there, Dodge—a miracle"(72).

Both Halie and Tilden allude clearly to the religious nature of this event. This is a play that makes the meaninglessness of conventional Christianity clear throughout. This is not the religion that can bring about the miracle of a renewed American dream. The minister, Dewis, is drunken, slyly lecherous and profoundly cynical ("God only hears what he wants to"[56]) and completely bankrupt spiritually: "I don't know what to do. I don't know what my position is. I just came in for some tea"(67). He neither understands Halie's need for belief nor her realization that we cannot live without it: "We can't not believe in something. We can't stop believing. We just end up dying if we stop. Just end up dead"(60).

Dewis's Christianity is one of meaningless platitudes that instead of facing and resolving problems, covers them up: "These are good people. All righteous people." His spiritual impotence is parallelled by Bradley's physical one. Bradley too wants to pretend all is well: "Nothing is wrong here! Nothing has ever been wrong! Everything's the way it's supposed to be. Nothing ever happened that's bad! Everything is allright here! We're all good people!"(63).

Dodge needs no sentimentalities to cover up his complete lack of belief as he tells Shelly: "Full of faith. Hope. Faith and hope. You're all alike. If it's not God then it's man. If it's not a man then it's a woman. If it's not a woman then it's the land or the future of some kind. Some kind of future"(52). He not only lacks faith in the possibility of transcendence but in humanity as well. "There's nothing a man can't do. You dream it up and he can do it. Anything"(53). Man, as exemplified by Dodge, is capable of any evil, and there is no reason to believe it will ever be different. "Now you think everything is gonna be different. Just 'cause the sun comes out," he mocks Shelly (52). The emptiness of this kind of religion is echoed by the meaninglessness of our culture. This is always in front of the audience's eyes in the form of the large TV set which never transmits a picture. The sound is never on, and no one ever seems to watch it but Dodge, who stares at its visionless screen. The jargon of advertisement comes between Halie's memories of youth and her articulation of the present. Her words are couched in travel advertisement words, "flaming sun, flamingos, bougainvilleas, palm trees"(14), and her recollections peopled with travel poster images, "everything was dancing with life. Everyone was dressed to the nines"(14). The recollections are merely remembered ads. She cannot even recall where they took place.

Shelly is the true outsider in this house of "rustic creepiness that verges into visionary madness among these characters who seem to be by Hyronimus Bosch superimposed on Grant Wood."[5] Her question, "What's happened to this family anyhow?"(54), sounds the theme of the play. She is frustrated in trying to make any sense of the strange menage. "There isn't any reason here! I can't find any reason for anything"(62).

Dodge senses Shelly's threat to his authority instantly. She is the only innocent and untainted among them. She is the one who unknowingly will force the secret, so long repressed, out into the open. Shelly understands the threat that the buried secret holds for her and the terror that lies behind the cliché of "turkey dinner and apple pie" (36). Her instinct for self-preservation is strong: "I'm fuckin' terrified. I wanna go"(36). The longer she stays, however, the greater becomes her despair at the betrayal of the American dream she shared. This is heightened by her realization that the family has become strangers in their own house, that they no longer correspond to the images and beliefs she has been taught: "For every name, I had an image. I really believed when I walked in through that door that the people who lived here would turn out to be the same people in my imagination. But I don't recognize any of you"(63). Shelly, however, is a survivor. She knows that she is powerless against Dodge and submits to his insulting sexual slurs. She calms him, puts him off his guard by assuming a seemingly nonthreatening domestic role: "I'll stay and cut the carrots and I'll cook the carrots and I'll do whatever I have to do to survive"(39). She sits on stage cutting large carrots, ironically emasculating him while he continues his sexual banter. Her rabbit coat, that both Tilden and Bradley want, provides the only warmth on stage throughout the play. They long for it like for the promise of love that has been so long denied.

Shelly will not be deterred from searching for reason and sense by Dodge's warning, "It's much better not to know anything"(34). Tilden understands the uselessness of pretense; understands that repression and silence can produce only death. Dodge refuses to face the sins that were committed: "I don't want to talk about anything. I don't want to talk about troubles or what happened fifty years ago or thirty years ago . . . "(25). Tilden warns him that silence will produce only death: "Well, you gotta talk or you'll die"(25). He senses that the answers lie in the past, in traditions that were once viable but have been debased and perverted, traditions that have now turned the land and its inhabitants toward death not life. The answer cannot lie in Dodge's senseless, unfeeling and unreflected action: "There's nothing to figure out. You just forge ahead"(25).

A Promise for the Future

Yet even Dodge knows that the emptiness of his present, the disasters that befell his three sons, are connected to the child he had killed: "My flesh and blood is buried in the backyard." Yet he continues to try to convince Tilden into believing that it all happened before he was born. Tilden, confused and burned out as he may be, will not forget: "I had a son once but we buried him"(37). He can still remember before he was "grown up," the days of innocence, the day before the unspeakable crime was committed. Tilden cannot forget. The memory of his child may have burned him out, but it still enables him to be the only one who sees the possibility of the land. The one who nurtured the child is the one who will make the earth fruitful again: "He'd walk all night out in the pasture with it. Talkin' to it. Singing to it. Used to hear him singing to it"(65). But Tilden could not protect the child from Dodge. "Little baby. Dodge killed it"(47). Tilden continues to mourn the child: "He [Dodge] is the only one who knows where it's buried. The only one. Like a secret treasure. Won't tell any of us. Won't tell me or mother . . ."(48).

This is the only time in the play that Tilden refers to Halie as mother—his mother and also the mother of his child. The mother who was unable to protect the true son, the savior. Like Eve, Halie bore the child in pain. It was Tilden's child that "begged to be born" (65) and that wanted to live, that would deny the heritage of Dodge's violence. It was the child that "wanted to be believed in"(65). Tilden is the image of the caring man who has returned to the world of the mother and has turned his back upon his father. Dodge commits infanticide for his patriarchal power was threatened: "Couldn't allow a thing like that to grow up in the middle of our lives"(65). The existence of the child promised a new world order which would have ended patriarchy's violent hegemony. This child had to be conceived through incest. How else are new races founded—with whom did Adam's son mate but with Eve?

But Dodge could not destroy the promise of the child. As Halie describes it: "You just gotta wait till it pops up out of the ground. Tiny little shoot. Tiny little white shoot all hairy and fragile. Strong though. Strong enough to break the earth even. It's a miracle . . ." (72).

The play ends like a miracle play with the symbol of the resurrection. The child is taken from the tomb, tended by its father and carried up, not to the patriarchal figure who lies dead on stage before us, but to the mother who is waiting above. *Buried Child* leaves the audience with hope for a revitalized America, for one that nourishes its children and holds the promise of the American dream once again.

Chapter Seven
Speaking in Tongues
Exploring the Inner Library

In the summer of 1978, Shepard returned to the collaborative process with which he had first worked in the late 1960s and with which he had experimented in 1977 in *Inacoma*. Shepard had known and respected Joseph Chaikin for over fifteen years and had approached him with the idea that they "build a piece together."[1] Chaikin came to San Francisco, and in three weeks they had created *Tongues*, a one-act play which, together with *Savage Love*, opened to enthusiastic reviews in November 1979 at the Public Theatre in New York. The two one-act plays explore the language of love and death.

Shepard drew together in these two short plays two themes that had concerned him during his fifteen years of playwriting—the relationship of music to words in the theater, and the inadequacy of language to express emotion. The collective title of the two plays is *Tongues*, which refers to both language and speech. While this seems to put Shepard—who chose the title—right in the midst of structural linguistics and its distinction between *la langue*, the abstract system of language, and *la parole*, the concrete, individual utterances we refer to as speech,[2] the playwright denies this. "Ideas like 'structuralism' are completely foreign to me."[3] Yet Shepard has long been fascinated by the very personal reference each writer has to language; a concern he has explored in "The Inner Library" article, which tries to express the inner territory which language attempts to chart. Despite Shepard's denials, his concern with the very personal associations that exist between words that a writer chooses brings his thinking close to that of La Saussure, who wrote of "the inner storehouse that makes up the language of each speaker."[4]

Shepard writes eloquently of what motivated him and Chaikin in the creation of the play:

If we talk seriously about the content of *Tongues* there's no point in trying to fix it into a concept of theatre. Our approach was always from the angle of experience. By that I mean "what is it like" to be in the multiplicity of situations that love calls us to. "What is it like" to be the beggar of love, the killer of love, etc. From there by deeply submerging oneself into the predicament, come all the questions, all the language, all the form. Not from the head. The head, at best, can only make up theories and theories don't hold water if experience defies them. This is the territory we were working in. I'm not at all interested in conceptual art. It's barren and void of true meaning. People are not moved toward their life by theories and concepts. If theatre is to have any meaning it must touch people where they live, not where they think they think. True thought only comes from opening to areas of experience that ordinary thought is too dull to grasp. So this opens lots of questions that appear very simplistic but have to be answered to. Mainly, what is experience and what is thought? To be more specific in regard to *Tongues* the questions were, what is the experience of love in domains that we felt hadn't been addressed. Moments of almost paralyzing doubt and wonder. What is the thought that can reach into that world and depict its mystery?[5]

What Shepard and Chaikin were trying to delve into is what Goethe called "incommensurable,"the relation between chaotic feeling and shaped artistic form.

Tongues

The first of the two one-act plays is *Tongues*. Its theme is death and dying. This focus came about partly from the creators' "interest in expressing extreme conditions, partly from an idea they had early on to structure the pieces as a fantasy of the past lives of a dying man—and partly from the fact that Chaikin literally was in heart failure."[6] In fact, when Chaikin returned to New York, he underwent open heart surgery. He has recovered from this ordeal and put in a stellar performance as the solo actor in the Public Theatre's production of the two monologues with music which make up *Tongues*. Chaikin recalls, "I was very weak when we were working on *Tongues*. Extremely sick, and I didn't know it."[7]

Since they presented the one-acter *Tongues* in the summer of 1978 at the Magic Theatre in San Francisco, Chaikin's weak physical condition determined the staging, which calls for the actor to sit almost motionless on stage: "an image suggesting illness and also somehow, a priest or medium through whom voices come."[8] The austere, static, onstage performance belies the peripatetic creation of the play, which was composed all over the city of San Francisco. "Sam likes egg foo yung, so we'd go to this Chinese restaurant, or we'd go to the park or to the zoo,"[9] Chaikin recollects. Since they worked all about the town, Chaikin remembers that deciding where they would eat became a daily ritual. Perhaps their daily conversations about food led Shepard once again brilliantly to use hunger as a metaphor. Shepard writes that they generalized "from that particular mundane hunger for food to many aspects of hunger, hunger of different levels. Fat people want more than just steaks."[10]

In *Tongues*, a piece described as being for voice and percussion, the character in a long "aria" speaks of a hunger that consumes him. "Nothing I ate could satisfy this hunger I'm having right now."[11]

This metaphor of spiritual hunger can be traced right through Shepard's plays. It becomes most agonizing in this long monologue delivered alone on a stage by a man barely moving a muscle. With the exception of the very short *Killer Head* (presented together with *Action* at the American Place Theatre), Shepard until now has explored humanity's problem of existential loneliness against a background of society where an attempt, even though unsuccessful, to communicate can be made. In *Tongues*, the aloneness of death is brilliantly brought to the audience's attention, as the actor feverishly tries to recall his life going back to birth; but the play becomes a death ritual.

Savage/Love

While the solitude in *Tongues* helps him learn the language of death, helps him administer his own death rites, the actor is equally alone in *Savage/Love*. It is an interesting commentary on Shepard's perception of love. Surely the language of love is difficult, if not impossible, to learn alone, in isolation. Despite his quest for attachment and commitment, the lover in *Savage/Love* sees love as more of a power struggle than anything else. The powerful image of killing that

Shepard uses focuses on the hatred inherent in love, on the doubt, competitiveness, and jealousy leading to its symbolic murder.

Music is an integral part of *Tongues*. The playbill for the Public Theatre's production states, "In one way, both of these collaborations are an attempt to find an equal expression between music and the actor. They are like environments where the words and gestures are given temporary atmospheres to breathe in through sound and rhythm." The plays are in fact structurally much closer to musical compositions than to plays. "Rather than having beginnings, middles, and ends, plots and consistent characters, they are built with themes that are stated, developed, and counterpointed."[12]

Sam Shepard has left behind, for the time being, his overwhelming involvement with the land and the dream, which he summed up in *Buried Child*, and has turned to the universals of death and love. The stark aloneness of the lover on a mattress crying out to a nonexistent partner: "Will you give me some part of yourself?" underlines Shepard's continuing concern for the individual's isolation on this cold star of an earth. Perhaps only a renewal of faith in the viability of the American dream can assuage the despair.

Chapter Eight

In the Bastard French Tradition: Arthur Kopit

The Beginning

By the time Arthur Kopit graduated Harvard in 1959, seven of his plays had been produced; four in major undergraduate productions, and three in private ones at Dunster House. An engineering major, he nevertheless was awarded a Shaw Traveling Scholarship for postgraduate study of the European theater. While traveling about western Europe, he wrote the play that was to make him a successful playwright at the age of twenty-three—*Oh, Dad, Poor Dad, Mamma's Hung You in the Closet and I'm Feelin' So Sad.*

He had written the play, he recalls, "to enter a playwriting contest at Harvard."[1] He did in fact win the $150 prize and a major undergraduate production. It created such a sensation at Harvard that it was moved to the Agassiz Theater in Cambridge, Massachusetts, where it was enthusiastically reviewed. "A bravely written, brilliantly written, exceedingly droll, almost constantly exhilarating play."[2] It came to the attention of the Phoenix Theatre in New York, where it was eventually produced almost two years later, ran for 454 performances, and won both the Vernon Rice Award and the Outer Circle Award.

Oh Dad, Poor Dad brought Kopit fame not only in the United States but in Europe as well. The play has been performed in England, France, and West Germany, where it has been particularly successful, and often played in repertory. Early success is often a mixed blessing: "Suddenly I was a successful playwright at 23 and there didn't seem much left to say."[3] In fact, Arthur Kopit never has had as much to say in such a short period of time as he had in those years at Harvard where he learned his craft—both in classes with Robert Chapman and Gaynor Bradish and on the college stage. The knowledge that his

66

plays would find an immediate audience may have made him so prolific: "The best thing for a writer is to know whom he's writing for, to have his own company of actors, and to have to turn out a play a year," he told a recent interviewer.[4] This has not been the case for Kopit. He has written but two major plays since *Oh Dad, Poor Dad*—*Indians* in 1968 and *Wings* in 1979, in addition to several one-acters.

The Harvard Plays

The remarkable polish of *Oh Dad, Poor Dad* was due in great part to what he had learned from his earlier Harvard plays. His first produced work was "The Questioning of Nick," which was written during spring vacation of his sophomore year for a Drama Workshop performance. "The next fall it won a college wide playwrighting contest and was performed on a more public scale,"[5] he recollects. The importance of that first step cannot be minimized: "My career was determined."[6] Unlike most of his subsequent plays, "The Questioning of Nick" was never rewritten. It also has the distinction of being the only realistic play Arthur Kopit has written. When he included it in a collection of his one-act plays, *The Day the Whores Came Out to Play Tennis*, published in 1965, he noted: "So, for those people who say to me, 'But when are you going to write a *real* play?'—here it is. (I assume when they say real, that what they mean is realistic.)"[7]

"The Questioning of Nick" is a well-crafted character study whose background draws on Kopit's own middle-class suburban experience as a high-school basketball player. The structure and language of the one-acter are shaped by the exploration of Nick's personality and its breakdown during a skillful police interrogation. It is a remarkably terse and disciplined work for a first effort.

His next play, produced by the Harvard Dramatic Club in 1956, showed Kopit's penchant for inventing titles—"On the Runway of Life You Never Know What's Coming Off Next." The play, which has never been published, is about a precocious fifteen-year-old boy who contrives to get himself adopted as an orphan by two good-hearted carnival strippers.

In "Don Juan in Texas" and "Across the River and Into the

Jungle," performed during the annual Dunster House Christmas week-end, he experimented with ever more wildly imaginative humor. In the cast of characters for "Don Juan in Texas" appear "2 cactus plants—that do not speak,"[8] which obviously foreshadowed the two Venus flytraps in *Oh Dad, Poor Dad*. Elements of parody which are so apparent in *Oh Dad, Poor Dad* can be seen in "Across the River and Into the Jungle," where polkadotted cannibals join in a duet with their victims in Noel Coward's "I'll See You Again." A parody of Hemingway's opening of *A Farewell to Arms* appears as the work of one of the characters in "Across the River and Into the Jungle": "In the late summer of that year we lived in a hut in a tree on a mountain that looked across the river and the plain and the valley to another mountain with a hut in a tree."[9]

His tutor at Dunster House, Gaynor Braddish, sees Kopit's undergraduate plays taking on a serious side in the summer before his senior year.[10] "Aubade," an hour-long monologue for an actress-dancer, explored the nature of love; "To Dwell in a Palace of Strangers," is a full-length play about a mysterious intruder from the past who returns to disrupt the life of a former friend.

The only other play of the Harvard period to be published is *Sing to Me Through Open Windows*,[11] "a delicate mood play about a boy, a magician and a clown."[12] In this work Kopit introduces the theme of impersonation and authenticity which he was to explore later in such plays as *Chamber Music* and *Indians*. The magician, Ottoman, is constantly searching for his own identity among his props. The stage directions read: "He now begins to pose before the mirror: a magician rehearsing the studied and aloof grandeur of his life's occupation" (60).

Kopit has always disavowed any influence the Theater of the Absurd has had on him: "I admire Beckett as one of the greats of the century but he has had no influence on me as far as I know."[13] *Sing to Me Through Open Windows*, however, does show Beckett's influence in both its structure and its language. The relationship between Ottoman and the Clown is strongly reminiscent of that of Hamm and Clov in *Endgame*.

We first see the Clown going "from window to window, repeating his ritual" (57) of opening the windows and shutters and looking up at the sky, very much as Clov does in *Endgame*. Ottoman puts on a golden robe and slippers and assumes a lord-servant relationship with the Clown who, we discover, is not a real clown at all but merely a man called Loveless wearing a clown costume. The two men play an endless game of assumed roles until Ottoman dies. "All my life it was someone else, standing there in the dark, watching me and laughing. I have vanished, Loveless. Suddenly I have vanished" (76).

The third character in *Sing to Me Through Open Windows* is a young boy who comes to visit them each year. He speaks of what he will remember when grown: "And then I remember. But strangely. For the words I remember are like the words of an unfamiliar language. And although I say them, some time later I will ask myself, *Now what was it again that you said to him . . . back there?*"(73). What he had told the Clown and Ottoman was: " 'I don't like it at home as much as I like it here,' he said. 'They're nice but they don't let me do what I really want. For instance, they would never understand about you.' And that was all that the boy said. And he truly believed it would be enough" (73).

The boy had come to stay with them and never go home again, stay in their world of illusion and constantly changing identities. But Ottoman releases him: "It's getting late now. I think you better go before it gets too late" (74). It was time to leave childhood dreams and enter into the reality of adult life.

In a 1965 interview Arthur Kopit spoke of *Sing to Me Through Open Windows*: "It's about the necessity of certain things dying to enable certain things to live. It deals with memory and time and it's not a comedy."[14]

The Holistic View

In a 1979 interview Arthur Kopit referred to his work as holistic: "I've been dealing with related issues for a long time: airplanes, flying, crashing, women pilots and women heroines."[15] His work, however, has had another unifying element that transcends the subject matter he cites. He has explored the nature of language and its function in the perception of reality throughout his plays: "I think the theater must have language at its core. I want to discover new ways of seeing things."[16] He has done this through means of parody in *Oh Dad, Poor Dad* in which he leads the audience to view our cultural myths in new ways; through pageant and sideshow in *Indians* in order to confront our historical myths, and through the exploration of the construction of speech and language itself in *Wings*.

Arthur Kopit sees the stage as "artificial—as a place to exaggerate, for grotesquery, not for the naturalistic."[17] The heart of his dramatic process is the use of language in such a way as to "shock us out of the anaesthetic grip our language maintains on our perception."[18] This permits us, then, to see our world anew by defamiliarizing that with which we are overfamiliar, "to creatively deform the usual, the normal, and so to inculcate a new childlike, non-jaded vision in us," wrote the Russian critic Shklovsky. "I want to show events as it wasn't. I want to distort because through distortion you arrive at clarity," Kopit told a 1969 interviewer.[19] The avant-garde theater had succeeded in creatively deforming the usual by the time that Kopit was writing *Oh Dad, Poor Dad*. It had created a style, a point of view that had itself become habitual and needed to be questioned. Thus the parody of *Oh Dad, Poor Dad*, using any number of literary words as a background, mounted in "A Bastard French Tradition," as the subtitle of the play tells us, makes us see the avant-garde and the problems it treated in new ways by "repeating it in a new incongruous context."[20]

The serious intent behind the hilarious onstage romp that *Oh Dad, Poor Dad* was can be seen in an article of Kopit's that appeared in the magazine *Theater Arts* in 1961, before *Oh Dad, Poor Dad* had opened in New York, but after the Harvard production had made him known. Titled "The Vital Matter of Environment," it delineated the young writer's theories of the relationship of the artist to his cultural millieu:

One can never wholly dissociate a work of art from its creative environment any more than one can separate its style from the traditions around it. . . . Tradition has always been the basis of all innovation, and always will be. . . . Style is related to tradition to the extent that it is representative of a cultural or social characteristic of its creative environment, and is itself characteristic to the extent that it has evolved from or rebelled against any of these.[21]

Relating the problem of creative environment directly to the American theater, Kopit decried its lack of tradition, which forced it to rely disproportionately on European dramatic innovations.

Chapter Nine

Oh Dad, Poor Dad, Mamma's Hung You in the Closet and I'm Feelin' So Sad

Few first plays have had as much critical success, caused more controversy, and earned as much money as *Oh Dad, Poor Dad*. Somewhere there is another funny play waiting to be written based on the divergent reviews and critiques the play garnered. The audiences, who kept the play running close to a year in New York and flocked to see it in several coast-to-coast road tours, seemed to be able to enjoy the burlesque comedy of the play without troubling themselves too much about the play's "meaning." It may be that a part of Kopit's success with the play was due to the bold and shrewd composition of the title,[1] which was as catchy in the many languages into which it was translated as it was in English. To wit: the Turkish translation "Ah Baba, vah Baba, Anam Asmis seni Dolaba, ne Usqunum Bilsen Buna."[2]

Reviewers from the daily press as well as such eminent literary critics as Martin Esslin were confused. Was *Oh Dad, Poor Dad* a spoof on Freudianism, a parody of the avant-garde theater, a scathing indictment of contemporary mores, or a projection of "a young man's feelings about a dominating mother who tries to deprive him of contact with the outside world?"[3] The answer to all these questions is simply "yes"; the play deals with all these themes, and in "A Bastard French Tradition" to boot.

The French tradition referred to in Kopit's subtitle is the one created by such playwrights as Beckett, Ionesco, Adamov, and Genet, and later labeled by critics "The Theatre of the Absurd." The definition of "absurd" came from Ionesco, "that which has no purpose, or goal, or objective."[4] Each of these writers wanted to express on the stage the basic senselessness and irrationality of all human actions. "They believe the theatre must confront audiences with that sense of isolation—the sense of man's being encircled in a void— which is an irremediable part of the human condition."[5] The themes of emptiness, frustration, change, despair, and death obsess these writers, and their plays are protests against the human condition. Exaggerating selected aspects of everyday reality in order to demonstrate its pointlessness has always been a favorite technique for the Absurdists, who saw their lives governed by the irrational, the inexplicable, and the nonsensical, and comedy was their natural medium. To them it was perhaps the only one that could give form to the irreconcilable forces that make up modern life. The comedy was, however, a special kind, the comedy of the grotesque: "This grotesque comedy is always conscious of suffering, is always close to tragedy. The name that best describes it is tragi-comedy."[6] As Ionesco put it: "It all comes to the same thing anyway; comic and tragic are merely two aspects of the same situation."[7]

Kopit made clear the importance of tradition to the creation of new form in his essay on the "Vital Matter of Environment." Lacking a viable American tradition against which to rebel, he turned to the "Bastard French" one, which had become as influential in America as in Europe. In *Oh Dad, Poor Dad* Kopit parodies both the overwhelmingly Freudian content of many American plays and the form of the Theater of the Absurd.

Oh Dad, Poor Dad tells the story of Madame Rosepettle, a fabulously wealthy widow who travels around the world with her ménage—the body of her husband, two venus flytraps, a silver piranha fish, and her son Jonathan, whom she tries to protect from life by keeping him away from the outside world. Rosalie, a teenage baby sitter, tries to seduce Jonathan on his mother's bed. After asserting himself enough to kill the fish and the man-eating plants, Jonathan panics and smothers Rosalie, covering the body with his "fabulous" coin, book, and stamp collections. The play ends with Mme Rosepettle's question to Jonathan, "What is the meaning of this?" (89),[8] Kopit's mocking challenge to the audience to find a serious interpretation to his seemingly mere parodistic joke.

The play's first line, "Put it in the bedroom" (15), immediately establishes the primacy of that room as the center of the action. When the audience discovers the "it" to be the father's coffin, which is to be placed next to the bed, a hilarious parallel to the romantic linkage of Eros to Thanatos is established. Reaching majority in an age when Freudian interpretations were used to explain all human motivations, where the bedroom literally was the center of all, the young Kopit is enjoying the tearing down of intellectual clichés that had become stifling. An era that had reduced *Hamlet* to a drama of the Oedipus complex, as in Olivier's famous film, was to be mocked by a father figure who falls out of the closet across the mother's bed, upon which a young girl is seducing the son. Another Polonius falls out from behind the arras onto incestuous sheets.

The writers of the Theater of the Absurd had rebelled against what they considered our preoccupation with psychology, which, they felt, denied theater's historical destiny—the portrayal of the mystery that passeth understanding. The young Kopit, too, rebelled against a theater in which all action was conceived to be psychologically plausible; he continues to support this point of view: "Plays should show inconsistencies, the way life does."[9]

The impossibility of communication between people is one of the favorite themes of the absurdists. Adamov, in describing how he came to write his first play, recalled: "One day I saw a blind man begging; two girls went by without seeing him, singing: 'I closed my eyes; it was marvellous!' This gave me the idea of showing on stage, as crudely, as visibly as possible, the loneliness of man, the absence of communication among human beings."[10]

Kopit plays with this lack of communication constantly in *Oh Dad, Poor Dad*. In the very first scene we see Mme Rosepettle's frustration in getting her orders carried out. "Oh, this talk is getting us nowhere," she complains (17). Jonathan is completely inarticulate; his stammering infuriates his mother, "Will you stop this infernal stammering" (19). But not only verbal communication fails the characters in *Oh Dad, Poor Dad*; feelings fare no better. Neither the Commodore nor Rosalie is able to reach either Mme Rosepettle or Jonathan emotionally or sexually. "Feelings are for animals, monsieur," Madame tells the Commodore sternly, "Words are for men"

(58). But we have just had ample evidence of the inefficacy of that human specialty. The books that are part of Jonathan's "priceless" collection are surrounded by clouds of dust, symbols of the bankruptcy of both the classic and romantic tradition against which the Absurdists reacted. Jonathan's "fabulous" coin and stamp collection proves to be equally bogus; the rarest of his coins, "a 1372 Javanese Yen Sen," was made by Mme Rosepettle herself.

The myth of the all-powerful mother who emasculates not only her sons but all men around her had become part of the American tradition. Beginning with Philip Wylie's exposé of "momism" in *A Generation of Vipers* (1955), a series of maternal monsters had invaded the American cultural scene. These threatened to turn upside down the time-honored fairy-tale characters and plots: "Tell me Commodore, how would you like to hear a little story? A bedtime story? A fairy tale full of handsome princes and enchanted maidens . . . ?" asks Mme Rosepettle (64). She proceeds to tell her version; the prince, Dad in person, was "as ugly as a humid day" (65), but he had the virtue of being so ineffectual as to be completely possessed by Madame. Rather than being antifeminist, as he was accused by, among others, Walter Kerr in his review of the play, Kopit saw through the basic power motive of the traditional fairy tale—the passive maiden waiting to be saved from the ogre and then possessed and owned by the handsome prince. In *Oh Dad, Poor Dad*, it is Jonathan who is being held captive by his mother, and the would-be rescuing prince is Rosalie, who wants to possess him herself: "I want you . . . all for myself" (84). Like the fairy-tale heroine of old, Jonathan's "skin is white as fresh snow" (72), and his mother is determined to keep him pure and safe from sexuality:

His skin is the color of fresh snow, his voice is like the music of angels, and his mind is pure. For he is safe, Mr. Roseabove, and it is I who have saved him. Saved him from the world beyond that door. The world of you. The world of his father. A world waiting to devour those who trust in it; those who love. A world vicious under the hypocrisy of kindness, ruthless under the falseness of a smile. Well, go on, Mr. Roseabove. Leave my room and enter your world again—your sex-driven, dirt-washed waste of cannibals eating each other up while they pretend they're kissing. (72)

Mme Rosepettle recalls another female figure that caused a stir on the world stage, Claire, the Old Lady, in Swiss dramatist Friedrich Durrenmatt's *Der Besuch der Alten Dame* [The Visit, 1958]. She, too, is fabulously wealthy and attempts to buy power and avenge herself on the man who had seduced her in her youth. Claire, who appears heavily veiled, as does Madame in the opening of *Oh Dad, Poor Dad*, turns out to be artificially put together not only with the help of cosmetics but by artificial limbs as well. Durrenmatt was here parodying a famous nineteenth-century German play by Heinrich von Kleist, *Das Käthchen von Heilborn* (1810). In this play the threatening female figure is unmasked in just such a fashion. Kleist was one of the nineteenth-century figures admired by the writers of the Theater of the Absurd. That Kopit was consciously alluding to his literary predecessors can be seen clearly during Mme Rosepettle's long "fairy tale" in which she articulates her revulsion toward men and sex:

And then, one night, when I was walking home I saw a man standing in a window. I saw him take his contact lenses out and his hearing aid out of his ear. I saw him take his teeth out of his thin-lipped mouth and drop them into a smiling glass of water. I saw him lift his snow-white hair off his wrinkled white head and place it on a gnarled wooden hat tree. And then I saw him take his clothes off. And when he was done and didn't move but stood and stared at a full-length mirror whose glass he had covered with towels, then I went home and wept. (65)

Our society's basic distrust of love and sexuality is immortalized by Kopit's mother figure walking along the beach at midnight searching for people lying on blankets and making love. "When she finds them, she kicks sand in their faces and walks on" (79). On the fateful night when Jonathan murders Rosalie, Madame had set a new record: "Twenty-three couples. I annoyed twenty-three couples, all of them coupled in various positions, all equally distasteful" (88).

The tyranny of parental love that Mme Rosepettle displays before us is another favorite theme of the Absurdists. Arthur Adamov, an influential French playwright of the 1950s, in two plays, *Les Retrouvailles* [The Recovered, 1952] and *Comme Nous Avons Eté* [As We Were, 1953], attacks the mother figure who is trying to keep the son from establishing an adult relationship with a woman. In *Comme Nous Avons Eté* the hero, who is about to get married, is gradually turned into a little boy by two women, mother and aunt. In *Les Retrouvailles* an amorphous mother figure forces the soon-to-be-married son into a state of physical dependency which culminates in his being pushed from the stage in a baby carriage. It is difficult to determine whether Kopit does a superior parody of that tradition, or whether the prize should be awarded to the BBC reviewer who seriously discussed Jonathan's fixation in the anal stage of development due to his mother's possessiveness. This critic found Jonathan's interest in collecting and preserving coins, stamps, and books an anal manifestation that made normal sex with Rosalie impossible, for the girl found those interests "stifling." Which, one supposes, makes Rosalie's Desdemona-like murder even more meaningful.

One of the reasons for *Oh Dad, Poor Dad*'s success was, according to several reviewers, the bizarre props the play employed..Not too many plays before *Oh Dad, Poor Dad* (or after it, for that matter) included characters like Rosalinda, the piranhafish, and two Venus flytraps in the cast of characters. They not only contributed to the bizarre hilarity of the play, but they were the perfect parody of one of the favorite dramatic techniques of the Theater of the Absurd. Its tendency to "externalize and project outward what is happening in the deeper recesses of the mind,"[11] as Martin Esslin called it. Kopit's man-eating plants that growl and try to grab Jonathan in a grip of death whenever he comes too close, and the silver piranha fish, who feeds only on pedigreed Siamese kittens, concretize the dangers of maternal love and the unresolved Oedipal conflict. In the same manner, Hamm's parents in Beckett's *Endgame*, who are confined in ashcans, concretize the subconscious to which Hamm has banished his past. A recent critical study of *Oh Dad, Poor Dad* saw the father's corpse as a concretization of the death of the "painfully Freudian aspects of the fantasy of American Dramatic tradition," and "the corpse of Freudian determinism worn out long ago."[12]

Another basic tenet of the Absurdists which Kopit found waiting to be mocked was their belief that the creating of a recognizable hero gave spurious, illusory meaning to an act which, like all human actions, is irreducibly absurd. Thus, in most plays in the Absurdist tradition, characters are types without individuality and often without names. The son has no individuality for his mother in *Oh Dad, Poor Dad*. The cast of characters gives him the name Jonathan, but Mme Rosepettle calls him Eduard or Albert or Robinson just as often. Characters are sometimes interchangeable in plays of the Theater of the Absurd; for example, in *Waiting for Godot*, Pozzo and Lucky change roles. In *Oh Dad, Poor Dad* Rosalie is almost a clone of Mme Rosepettle, just as manipulative and predatory in her attempt to capture Jonathan as Madame had been in her pursuit of the father.

The conviction that the theater must express the senselessness and irrationality of human action was held by most of the writers of the Theater of the Absurd. Kopit works with this belief in *Oh Dad, Poor Dad* as well. "You take the time to build a telescope that can see for miles, then there's nothing out there to see. Mother says it's a lesson in Life," stammers Jonathan sadly (37). He is obsessed with airplanes and the idea of flying and lives in the hope that someday the plane he had once seen would return. At the end of the play, after he has killed Rosalie, the stage directions read: "An airplane is heard flying in the distance. Jonathan scans the horizon frantically. The plane grows nearer. Jonathan follows it with his telescope. It flies overhead. It begins to circle about. Wildly, desperately, Jonathan waves his arms to the plane. . . . It flies away" (89).

Although Kopit uses the image of the plane in *Oh Dad, Poor Dad* in the framework of the parodistic mockery of the Theater of the Absurd, there is no doubt that Kopit, like Jonathan, is fascinated by flying. The figure of the aviatrix appears in *Chamber Music* and again in *Wings*. In the same way, he returns to the problem of human communication in *Wings*.

Kopit parodies not only the "French Tradition" in *Oh Dad, Poor Dad*, as well as the Freudian overemphasis of the times, but two giants of the American stage as well. Venus flytraps appear not only in *Oh Dad, Poor Dad*, but in Tennessee Williams's *Suddenly Last Summer* as well. The relationship between Jonathan and Mme Rosepettle has many parallels to that of the fragile Sebastian and his mother in the Williams play. A recent critical article pointed out that the scene that Mme Rosepettle uses as a setting for her tryst with the Commodore— two flickering candles, a bottle of champagne, a flower vase with one wilting rose protruding, a Viennese Waltz playing softly in the background—might have been designed by Blanche DuBois herself.[13] The symbiotic bond between Mme Rosepettle and Jonathan, with its sexual overtones, could not help but remind audiences of the agonizing relationship between mother and son in O'Neill's *Long Day's Journey into Night*. In case this allusion to O'Neill is not pointed enough, Kopit underscores it in his use of language, which is strongly reminiscent of the great writer's style: "If the sunset over Guanobaca Bay were not so full of magenta and wisteria blue I'd leave this place tonight. But the sunset is full of magenta and wisteria blue, to say nothing of cadmium orange and cerise, and so I think I'll stay" (27).[14]

One critic called *Oh Dad, Poor Dad* a play that might have been written in collaboration with "Samuel Beckett, Sophocles, Ronald Firbank, Edgar Allan Poe, Salvador Dali and Robert Benchley."[15] He might have added Racine or Corneille to the names of Kopit's collaborators for Kopit indeed created a "pseudoclassical" play that strictly conforms to the three unities.

Oh Dad, Poor Dad not only made Kopit well known around the Western world, but afforded him at a very young age the financial security to devote his life to writing.

Chapter Ten

The Madhouse as Metaphor and *The Cherry Orchard* Revisited

The Madhouse as Metaphor

The madhouse as metaphor for a world devoid of meaning, inhabited by individuals who have fled the reality of their lost identities and self-estrangement into insanity, was popular in the 1960s. It was used successfully by Peter Weiss, the German living in Sweden, in *The Persecution and Assassination of Jean-Paul Marat As Performed by the Inmates of the Asylum of Charenton Under the Direction of The Marquis de Sade*, and the Swiss Friedrich Duerrenmatt, in *The Physicists*. Arthur Kopit conceived the idea of theatrically actualizing the environment in which contemporary humanity found itself, at the same time as *Oh Dad, Poor Dad*. "It was not begun however until the late spring of 1962. It was finished that summer," he later explained.[1]

Chamber Music was previewed in 1963 in New York, but the author canceled the opening in order to rewrite the one-act play, which was not to be seen in New York until 1971. It was published, however, in 1965 in the collection of Kopit's one-act plays: *The Day the Whores Came Out to Play Tennis*.

Chamber Music takes place in a room in an asylum which is furnished like a boardroom with a large horseshoe-shaped table. Around this table nine women inmates meet to conduct the "Sixth Annual Meeting of the duly-Elected Grievance and Someday-Governing Committee of Wing Five, Women's Section" (9). The women, who all have assumed different identities and are acting out their secret compulsions, have met to discuss "the record of hostile occurrences" which all the women have sensed. Unable to find reasons for them, they conclude: "In short, then, these reports all prove that no source can be found for the various feelings of hatred, hostility, jealousy, belligerency and revenge known to exist. The conclusion then. The source must come from *outside* our ward. Or, in other words, the Men's Ward! Which none of us have ever seen. And is therefore, most likely" (22).

In order to prevent the perceived hostility of the Men's Ward from becoming actualized, the women develop a plan to frighten their enemy, who they know is stronger than they. They plan to convince the men of their superior strength: "Just think of this: a body for argument's sake, mine, let us say sent in the dead of night, arriving at the Men's Ward first thing in the morning, our signatures attached. Well! I ask you, would that be a warning or wouldn't it? Would that frighten the Men's Ward or wouldn't it? Would that be a show of strength, a show of power, of intention? Or wouldn't it!" Should the men still not be convinced of the women's superior power: "If that didn't work, we could send another one in the afternoon, then perhaps another the following morning. Oh, yes, they'd soon get the point. They'd soon realize that they could be next" (31). The women carry out their ritual murder and, their energy spent, retreat into quiescence.

The play takes place against a backdrop of businesslike, sensible normality which the action belies. The madness of the situation is underlined by the parliamentary order in which the women carry off their futile action. The image of the perceived rationality and logic of political leaders coldly and "sensibly" planning courses of action that ultimately lead only to the destruction of human life, and perhaps the world, is conjured up. That Kopit means the audience to feel the significance of the menace of the women's actions can be seen in the play's ending. The last speech of the Assistant, the ineffectual authority figure unable to prevent the compulsive acting out of hostility, is filled with threatening signs of a world without reason: "From the moment I got up, something in the air. Like the women outside, for instance, lined up in their rocking chairs and laughing away. Well, they've done that before, of course. But yet . . . just laughing away. . . . What is it they claim now? Oh, yes. That the sun has gone forever and now there will be only night" (38).

Kopit has chosen women to show the futility or impossiblity of meaningful human action. The women are listed in the cast of characters by their external trappings: Woman who Plays Records, Woman in Safari Outfit, Woman with Notebook, Girl in Gossamer Dress, Woman in Aviatrix's Outfit, Woman in Queenly Spanish Garb, Woman in Armor, Woman with Gavel. During their discussion it becomes clear which role each of these women has assumed. With the exception of the Woman who Plays Records and thinks she is Mrs. Mozart, all the other inmates have chosen to play roles of nontraditional heroic women: the explorer Osa Johnson; Gertrude Stein; Pearl White, the silent movie star who specialized in adventurous girl heroines; Amelia Earhart, Queen Isabella of Spain, St. Joan, and Susan B. Anthony. Only by play-acting have these women been able to take active societal roles and lead authentic lives in a society which had permitted them to define their own identities in only male terms.

Thus the characters in *Chamber Music* are doubly unfree. They are confined by their roles, and they are patently not free, for they are inmates of an asylum and thus locked away from society. The hostility they feel may be the projection of their own hatred of those who imprison them—be it the men who are the necessary opposite against whose image they attempt to define themselves, or the society which incarcerated them. Yet the enemy in *Chamber Music* seems to have little more power than they have. The men remain but shadows in the women's imagination and the authority figures— the Man in White and the Assistant—are ineffectually reduced to mumbling trite appeals to the inmates' decorum. The only action that seems to have any promise of meaning to the women is the ritual of killing. Anne Murch has pointed out that the murder of the Woman in Aviatrix's Outfit was a holy murder, ritualized and institutionalized—institutionalized because of its political necessity for the group's survival, and ritualized because it is directed against a perceived outsider.[2] "Amelia Earhart" had set herself apart by her show of rationality.

Yet the murder will have no effect on the outside world; it will make no difference in the women's situation. At best it will have released tension from an unbearable situation. It was a murder that would be qualified as a sociologically dysfunctional type of ritual whose aim is to act out the rejection of the existing social order as unfit for the individual to live in.[3] Generally, anthropologists have shown us that ritual is meant to be functional—a means by which a person or a group that has outgrown its societal role is led to take up new roles which can be integrated into society. The women in *Chamber Music* are doubly outside of society—they are deemed mad, and they can find no roles in society to fill which would enable them to live authentic lives.

In their interaction, the women show their fear of overt rebellion against an authority which has the power to prevent them from enjoying the little that is allowed them. The frustration engendered by their helplessness is directed against each other, and they seize every opportunity to torment one another. Is humanity that feels more and more powerless and manipulated by forces that no longer seem to have any meaning doomed to torture each other endlessly in a world "they never made?"

Kopit actualized the hopelessness of the situation theatrically throughout *Chamber Music*. From the moment that the Mozart Quartet in F Major that we hear at the very beginning of the play is turned off, we leave the world of order and rationality and enter the province of the meaningless and the absurd. In the Quartet, the voices of the instruments, while divergent and individual, produce harmony; in the asylum the voices are strident, producing discord. The impossibility of human communication is concretized by the Woman in Armor who slams down her visor and thus cuts off all communication with the outside world. The inappropriateness and ineffectuality of the trite formulas spouted by the authority figures is underlined by the great display of the passing of cigarettes among the women who ceremoniously puff on unlit cigarettes—matches being forbidden to the inmates.

If, as Ionesco states, the comic and the tragic are but reverse sides of the same thing, then Arthur Kopit, who worked with the comic in *Oh Dad, Poor Dad*, viewed the world through a tragic prism in *Chamber Music*.

The Cherry Orchard Revisited

With *The Day the Whores Came Out to Play Tennis*, Arthur Kopit returned to the playful uses of parody which had proved so successful in *Oh Dad, Poor Dad*. Not only the outrageousness of the titles connect the two plays, but their approach as well. If *Oh Dad, Poor Dad* was written in the "Bastard French Tradition," then *The Day the Whores Came Out to Play Tennis* was written in the "Bastard Russian Tradition." In the only critical analysis of the play, David L. Rinear shows how closely Kopit has parodied *The Cherry Orchard* in *The Day the Whores Came Out to Play Tennis*.[4] The theme of the Chekhov play is the loss of power of one social class to another and the subsequent devaluation of the values of the former ruling group. The disintegration of the Russian aristocracy is represented by Lyubia, her family, and their prized cherry orchard, which is literally destroyed at the end of the play. The five men of the executive committee of the Cherry Valley Country Club in Kopit's play are trying to protect their island of privilege and prosperity against a group of women who have taken over the club's tennis courts. The women's attire and their behavior make the committee believe they are whores. The five men who all have Russian names spend the entire play discussing the problem, attacking each other, but taking no positive action to ameliorate the situation.

Just as the stage setting for the first act of Chekhov's *The Cherry Orchard* is "A room that is still called the nursery," Kopit's play is set in "a room that is still called the nursery."[5] In both plays the time is toward dawn and although the sun is up and it is spring, there is frost. Kopit has made the analogies between *The Day the Whores Came Out to Play Tennis* and *The Cherry Orchard* clear throughout his play. The language his characters use to delineate the problem they must face is a parody of the great Russian writer:

The clubhouse grew older. And we grew older in it. And as we did we guarded it from others; shared it with our friends. The bridle path. The pool. The fairways, the tennis courts. The lake. The dance hall! The dining hall (with its great floral curtains, its soft green wall). The steam room, too. Yes . . . and the gymnasium. The solarium! The movie theatre! The bar! We spent our time here. And we enjoyed ourselves. Then. Today these women came. These . . . strange women. . . . And cut the telephone wires. Well. So. Here we are. The committee. With nothing to do. And that's the crying shame of it. Nothing to do. But sit in the Nursery like little children . . . and watch what we built collapse all about us. (140)

But Arthur Kopit uses this parody of Chekhov as more than an amusing literary pastiche. He uses it again to make the point that America is lacking in traditions and values against which to measure the present. The Russian aristocrats of *The Cherry Orchard* were genuine Russian aristocrats and the values they represented were authentic ones even if they were no longer viable. But Kopit's characters are searching for authenticity. The country-club manners they try to assume are not theirs. They are pathetic copies of the country-club set which would never accept the Russian Jews who make up the committee. Their attempts are as unsuccessful and bogus as the magic tricks Old Gayve is constantly trying out. The members try to impress the club's butler that they know how to dress and behave. Their actions and appearance on stage belie these endeavors:

I wish, when you called, you'd told me we'd have this much time. I'd have found a proper shirt somewhere. Florence, you see, threw my tuxedo shirt into the hamper as soon as we got home. I don't wear a shirt more than once. It isn't right. Wearing a wrinkled shirt is rude. Well, no sooner was my shirt in the hamper than you called, telling me to come back. Now of course everyone here will say, "In such a case you should have put on another type of shirt." But I'm afraid that isn't true. One must only wear a tuxedo shirt with a tuxedo. And certainly never a wrinkled one. So, I put on a pajama top. You see? . . . Under here . . . a pajama top. That way, if some passer-by saw me, he'd know something was wrong—an emergency—"Look at Alexander Ratscin! He had to get dressed in a hurry," he'd say . . . and wouldn't think I simply had no taste in clothes (107).

If Chekhov's characters are unable to do anything but passively await their fate because their energy and values have been sapped and outdated, Kopit's characters are unable to act because their values are artificial and phony. Thus again Kopit has used parody to emphasize his concern over in-authentic American traditions. It was not until his second major play, *Indians*, that he found a truly American tradition with which to work.

When Tyrone Guthrie, with the help of a Rockefeller grant, offered to stage *The Day the Whores Came Out to Play Tennis*, the future looked bright for this one-act play. But the University of Minnesota, where Guthrie was working, refused public performances for the workshop production. The young author angrily charged the university with censorship and withdrew his play: "One of the things that benefits a playwright is an audience. Though the University has denied censorship, it is censorship in its most insidious form. It is also deceit," charged Kopit in a *New York Times* interview (January 13, 1964).

When *The Day the Whores Came out to Play Tennis* opened in New York at the Players Theatre in March 1965, Michael Smith in the *Village Voice* sagely commented that the play suffered because reviewers expected a major work from an established writer rather than a one-act play from a talented young man who happened to strike it rich the first time around.

Chapter Eleven

A Myth Reconsidered:
Indians

The Genesis

It is not often that artists can pinpoint the exact moment the idea for a work occurred to them. But Arthur Kopit remembers clearly the impetus for writing *Indians*. It was in March 1966, when he read of a statement by General Westmoreland, the Commander-in-Chief of American forces in Vietnam, expressing regret at a particularly senseless slaughter of civilians. The general was quoted as having said that our hearts go out to innocent victims. "I knew almost instantly, while listening to Ives' 4th, that I would write a play that would explore what happens when a social and political power imposes itself on a lesser power and creates a mythology to justify it, as we did with the Indians, as we've tried to do in Vietnam,"[1] he recalled.

He continued his recollection: "I just sort of went berserk. I thought no, our hearts do not go out to the innocent because there's something wrong. I didn't think Vietnam was the real problem but a symptom of something which went back much farther. It dealt with obfuscation. Then suddenly I thought that it was Indians and the white man, it was part of a struggle in which we'd been fighting throughout history against people whom we conceived as being spiritually, morally, economically and intellectually our inferiors. We imposed our will on them and then justified our will morally in terms of some godly sensation that we felt was for a general and moral good."[2]

Indians was first produced by the Royal Shakespeare Company on July 4, 1968. Kopit chose to premiere the play in London, "because of its strong political underpinnings." "Even before I started to write it," he went on, "I know it would have to be produced in England, so that it could have a life; so that it would be done in theaters around the world. In New York it wouldn't have been judged on its own merits. Not in 1968. And the production we planned was very expensive, so a New York opening would have been far too risky."[3]

The Uses of Myths

John Lahr calls *Indians* not so much a "protest play as a process play,"[4] an exploration of the cosmeticizing of our history, of the creation of a mythology which enabled us to transform the brutal realities of the conquest of the West into the realization of the hopes and dreams that the West had always promised. It is a process that de Tocqueville had observed in the nineteenth century: "The Americans have accomplished this twofold purpose (of annihilating the Indians and denying him his rights) with singular felicity, tranquilly, legally, philanthropically without shedding blood and without violating a single principle of morality in the eyes of the world. It is impossible to destroy men with more respect for the laws of humanity."[5]

What Kopit was interested in was to place the Vietnam War in the larger context of American history and American mythology. It is one of the properties of myths and mythical thinking that it can create a synthesis of the seemingly unresolvable opposites of human behavior and accepted ethical codes. Thus by means of myths we can create our own reality: "America becomes its own image. A Frankenstein monster becoming its own creator, forgetting it made the whole thing up. It's how we can equate Vietnam with Korea when there is such a clear difference."[6]

The primary function of myth, however, has always been to validate an existing social order by putting an aura of sanctity about the status quo, thus justifying its conservation as all important.

According to the French anthropologist Claude Levi-Strauss, "In our own societies, history has replaced mythology and fulfills the same functions, that for societies without reading and writing and without archives the aims of mythology is—to ensure that as closely as possible—the future will remain faithful to the present and to the past."[7]

Thus the function of what Lahr calls our American penchant for "historical amnesia" can be seen to be the basic function of all mythic thinking. "At the core of the American myth is the inherent goodness and altruism of Americans. Whatever we do is for the ultimate good of those to whom we do it, because our greater moral strength and our superior mental and technical qualifications enable us to see further and deeper than the primitive people."[8] According to the historian Bruce Curtis, this myth has enabled us to lie to ourselves that our motives and ends were pure even though the means used to achieve them were tainted. Kopit clearly wanted to show the dangers inherent in this thinking. "The purpose of the play was to create a fresh feeling for the confusions of history, the amorphousness of history, and hopefully, to put the Vietnamese situation into a context of American history and American method,"[9] he explained.

Kopit thus uses history in order to draw from it certain illuminating events and ideas that would enable him, by reinterpreting these events and ideas in contemporary terms, to further his argument that ". . . Vietnam had to happen, that historically it was inevitable."[10] He makes no attempt to reproduce realistically historical happenings. Instead the playwright uses a variety of theatrical techniques to create what he called "a mosaic, a counterpoint of memory and reality."[11]

Curtis pointed out that perhaps the nonrealistic, nonnaturalistic technique is the only one that will do because "certain American realities are surreal. All that *Indians* needed, since it is so centrally concerned with America's Vietnam experience, was to have a Cavalry colonel destroy an Indian village in order to save it or to have Ol' Time President announce that the cavalry's movement into Indian territory was not really an invasion."[12]

Far too sophisticated to attempt to write a straight propaganda play to carry his message, the structure of Kopit's argument may have come to him at the same time as his theme. Vera Jiji explains, "At the moment of hearing Westmoreland's statement, he happened to be listening to a symphony by Charles Ives in which chamber music is played against distorted marching band music. In the contemporary symphony, the grave, sweet, measured assonance of the chamber music clashes ironically with the harsh dissonance of the military band."[13] The "sweet assonance" of the myth of our inherent altruism clashing with the dissonance of American military policies is dramatically shown in *Indians*, creating the kind of discomfort in the audience that is caused by being confronted by facts and realities long suppressed.

Another one of the properties of a myth is its observability under different transformations. One of Kopit's themes in *Indians* is that the phenomenon we were seeing on our TV sets—the Vietnam War—was not an isolated event, but had occurred in our historical past before, was in fact a continuing process in our history.

Transformation or impersonation is as inherent to the theater as it is to mythmaking. In traditional mythology, deities personified natural phenomena; in the secular mythology of history, mortals impersonate what they are thought to be. Kopit uses the duplicity, disguises, and impersonations that were used to create the myth of the Wild West, that often were at the core of the so-called historical facts, as the building blocks from which he constructed *Indians*. Show business has become our age's professional mythmaker, and thus Kopit chose to express his concerns with the visual metaphor of Buffalo Bill's Wild West Show. He used this as the starting point for "getting at the levels of illusion that camouflage the real facts and figures of the American heritage."[14] William Cody's attempt to package the American heritage commercially as "ShowBiz" was but the first of many of such endeavors. Kopit was drawn to Cody as the archetypal American hero who personifies both America's genuine good intentions and their ultimate corruption:

Buffalo Bill's stroke of genius was to get real people from Western history into his show, to get Sitting Bull to play himself, to get the Indians to play themselves, to recreate Custer's Last Stand, to show the Deadwood Stage. Of course, he would alter the facts. He would ride in to save the Deadwood Coach, and so Buffalo Bill became involved in the dilution of history because it made what happened into fiction and he used real people to fictionalize themselves.[15]

The Threat to Authenticity

The second major theme of *Indians* is the threat to authentic existence and personal integrity presented by constant self-impersonation. This is brought about by the perception of self only through the eyes of others. In the play, the Indians' as well as Cody's authenticity is destroyed by the mythicizing process of impersonation. The Indians, as do all minorities, after a while take on the values of the majority and begin to see themselves as inferior. This, of course, is the ultimate denial of their freedom—the freedom to see themselves on their own terms rather than in those of the white man. William Cody/Buffalo Bill's authenticity is threatened as well; he can no longer distinguish the difference between the original William Cody and the mythical Buffalo Bill. His greatest fear, thus, is that he might die with his makeup on, die as unauthentically as he had lived: "Scared . . . not . . . so much of dyin' . . . but . . . dyin' wrong. Dyin' . . . in the center of my arena with . . . makeup on" (88).[16] It is a fear that is shared by the bravest, most genuine of the Indians, Sitting Bull, who is terrified that he had unconsciously accepted the white man's vision of himself so fully that this false image had become the only heritage he could pass on to his children: "I agreed to go onto the reservation. I was standing in front of my tribe, the soldiers leading us into the fort. And as we walked, I turned to my son, who was beside me. 'Now,' I said, 'you will never know what it is to be an Indian, for you will never again have a gun or pony . . .' Only later did I realize what I'd said. These things, the gun and the pony—they came with you. And then I thought, ah, how terrible it would be if we finally owe to the white man not only our destruction, but also our glory . . ." (88).

Working with the metaphor of the Wild West Show, Kopit structured *Indians* into thirteen scenes which, by means of flashbacks, deal with roughly twenty-four years of American history—from the surrender of Geronimo in 1860 to the Wounded Knee Massacre in 1880. Kopit supplies at the beginning of the printed text of the play the important events and dates of William Cody's life, which are titled "Chronology for a Dream."

The scenes describe the destruction of the Indian tribes and the loss of Cody's integrity and authenticity by more or less alternating between portrayal of events in the real world and those in the mythicized world of the Wild West Show. It has been pointed out that "each world makes an explicit or implicit comment upon the other."[17] The first and the last scene use the same artificial visual props, emphasizing the circular structure of the play. The play uses the musical form of the rondo, in which the themes and conventions are introduced in an overture, developed contrapuntally, and recapitulated in a coda.[18]

The theatrical tradition upon which Kopit leans most heavily is the Brechtian epic. The purpose and technique of Brechtian theater is to make the audience aware of historical processes by showing them, in a theatrical way, to be changeable and man-made, rather than immutable and natural. The audience attending such a performance is not to be lulled into accepting a comfortable, passive experience but is to be exhorted to think and draw its own conclusions from the "evidence" presented. Thus the dramatic illusion that what was presented on stage was reality rather than play-acting had to be broken constantly by the process Brecht called *Verfremdung* ("estrangement"). The audience had to be prevented from giving in to the temptation of accepting what was happening on stage at face value. Thus the very first visual impact of *Indians* is "three large glass cases, one holding a larger-than-life-size effigy of Buffalo Bill in fancy embroidered buckskin. One, an effigy of Sitting Bull dressed in a simple buckskin or cloth, no headdress, little if any ornamentation. The third case contains some artifacts: a buffalo skull, a blood-stained Indian shirt, an old rifle" (1). The first aural impact the audience experiences according to the stage directions is "Strange music from all about. Sense of dislocation."

The stage is set for the appearance of Buffalo Bill, who wears the same costume as his effigy in the case and is riding a "glorious white artificial stallion with wild, glowing eyes" (2). The theatricality and artificiality to come are concretized for the audience by the open-framed oval fence that rises and encloses to frame the action of the play. The deliberate unreality of the setting underlines the distortion of the white man's view of both himself and of the Indians. The stage directions make this amply clear: "Then a great smile on his face, Buffalo Bill begins to tour the ring, one hand lightly gripping the reins, the other proudly waving his big Stetson to the unseen surrounding crowd. Surely it is a great sight; the horse prances, struts, canters, dances to the music, leaps softly through the light. Buffalo Bill effortlessly in control of the whole world, the universe, eternity" (2).

Both Buffalo Bill and the disembodied voice that is heard immediately put the audience in the role of jurors—jurors who will be asked to come to some sort of conclusion about the figure of William Cody/Buffalo Bill, jurors whose vision of American history is to be altered by what they are about to see. The audience is made aware of the conflict within Cody between his public self as Buffalo Bill, the mythic hero, and his private self, William Cody, the friend of the Indians. His growing realizations that the part he played in creating and selling the illusion of the Wild West had hastened the destruction of the Indians is shared by the audience. We see Indians appearing around the outside of the ring: "The horse senses their presence and shies; Buffalo Bill, as if realizing what it means turns in terror" (5). These ghostly Indians have come to haunt Cody, and his attempt to protect his public image from his growing guilt about his acquiescence to the selling of the American heritage, is manifested: "I am a fine man. And anyone who says otherwise is wrong . . . My life is an open book; I'm not ashamed of its bein' looked at! . . . I'm sorry this is very . . . hard . . . for me t' say. But I believe I . . . am a . . . hero. A GODDAM HERO!" (5)

The second scene introduces us to the plot that parallels Cody's gradual loss of dignity and authenticity—the destruction of the tribes. Based on the historical fact of a United States Commission visiting Standing Rock Reservation to investigate Indian grievances in 1886, the scene shows how the white man forced the Indian to play the part of recalcitrant, ignorant children: "Indians! Please be assured that this committee has not come to punish you or take away any of your land but only to hear your grievances, determine if they are just. And if so, remedy them. For we, like the Great Father, wish only the best for our Indian children" (7). Sitting Bull, dressed "simply," authentically, as was his effigy, in contrast to Buffalo Bill's costume, narrates the history of his tribe. The depth of his humiliation is symbolized by his appearance, impersonating himself, in the show of "My friend, William Cody" (7). Cody is seen as genuinely concerned in helping the Indians survive, yet his word is juxtaposed with Sitting Bull's recollection of appearing in the Wild West Show in "exchange for some food and little clothing. A beautiful horse that could do tricks" (8).

The young Indian, John Grass, who had been to the white man's school, is asked by Sitting Bull to state the Indians' demands. He is dressed "in a black cutaway many sizes too small for him. He wears an Indian Shirt" (9), concretely showing his discomfort in living half in one culture, half in the other. Grass's delineation of the Indians' grievances clarifies the inevitability of the clash between them and the white man, and the hopelessness of the Indians' plight is movingly portrayed in Sitting Bull's vain prayer for the return of the buffalo.

This leads directly to the third scene, which takes us back to the period of 1869–1872 when William Cody began to assume the legendary mantle of Buffalo Bill. It is a scene of almost continuous impersonations, beginning with the Indians impersonating wounded and dying buffaloes. Barbara Hurrell sees the meaning of these impersonated buffaloes being shot in their eyes in the existential notion of *le regard* articulated by Sartre.[19]

In existential thought all that is not "self" is considered to be the "other." Much of the alienation and despair common to existentialism comes from this separation of the self from all else. And, since the existential goal is to act freely, this freedom is always under attack by the "other." Thus Sartre tends to see all interpersonal or interracial relationships as a never-ending struggle to "seduce" or force a desired self-image upon the "other" and vice versa. Victory, in a sense, is when you can "look at" without being "looked at."

Thus the Indians in impersonating buffaloes shot in the eyes underline their symbolic defeat by the white man on one level, and the physical impossibility of Indian life without the buffalo on another. This is immediately reinforced by Cody's realized dream of killing 100 buffaloes with 100 bullets, which led to the misery we heard about in the second scene. Guilt at this slaughter for exhibition purposes is already manifesting itself: ". . . these critters are getting damn hard to find . . . Not like the ol' days when I was huntin' em fer the railroads. (He laughs, gazes down at one of the buffaloes. Pause. He looks away, squints as if in pain" (12).

He sees his old friend Spotted Tail and, in telling him of his plans for the future, clearly expresses the two motives of his actions, which will lead inevitably to the destruction of his own integrity:

Well, my plan is t' help people. Like you, fer instance. Or these people I'm with. More . . . even . . . than that, maybe. And, and, whatever . . . it is I do t' help, for it, these people may someday jus' possibly name streets after me. Cities. Counties. States! I'll . . . be as famous as Dan'l Boone! . . . An' somewhere, on top of a beautiful mountain that overlooks more plains 'n rivers that any other mountain, there might even be a statue of me sittin' on a great white horse, a-wavin' my hat t' everyone down below, thankin' 'em, fer thankin' me, fer havin' done . . . whatever . . . it is I'm gonna . . . do fer 'em all. (14)

His desire for glory prepares the audience for the entrance of Ned Buntline, a dime-novel writer, under whose coaching Cody begins to fashion the impersonation of his self. Buntline supplies the rationale for the development of the myth: ". . . de West is changin' Right? Well, people wanna know about it. Wanna feel . . . part o' things. I think you're what they need. Someone t' listen to, observe, identify wid . . . I think you could be de inspiration o' dis land. . . ." (18–19).

The Grand Duke is inspired to play Buffalo Bill and actually succeeds in killing Spotted Tail, who has been passed off as an authentic bloodthirsty Comanche. The theatricality of the scene is kept in the foreground with the "dead" Spotted Tail addressing the audience, asserting his authenticity and identity: "My name is Spotted Tail. My father was a Sioux, my mother, part Cherokee, part Crow. No matter how you look at it, I'm just not a Comanche" (22).

Cody falsifies Spotted Tail's final speech to the Grand Duke in a last act of betrayal. The scene ends with Buffalo Bill "dizzily gripping his head," realizing that his attempt to preserve the consistency of his newly created legend will force him to corrupt himself.

The fourth scene brings the action back to the Commission Hearing and Cody's desperate attempt to save the lives of Sitting Bull's tribe. He vainly tries to impress upon the senators the importance of these Indians who were the last to attempt to preserve their authenticity.

This is immediately followed by a theatrical scene depicting the caged Geronimo, forced to impersonate what he once was, "The Most Ferocious Indian Alive." It graphically depicts the Indian warrior's ultimate humiliation in the service of the creation of Buffalo Bill's mythic self: "Buffalo Bill, in his fancy buckskins, enters unnoticed by Geronimo, drum roll. He opens the cage door and walks inside . . . slowly, Buffalo Bill walks toward him. He stops just short of the Indian. Then defiantly turns his back" (28).

This symbolic scene of degradation is followed by one which takes the action back to the Commission's investigation. During the discussion it becomes clear that the treaties signed by the Indians were indeed a sham. They were a masking of the true intent of the white man to deprive the Indians of their land. Buffalo Bill's ineffectiveness in mitigating the situation becomes more and more evident, as he pleads with the Indians: "Look, don't you understand? These men are your only hope. If you turn away from them, it's like . . . committing suicide" (31).

The seventh scene of *Indians* is not only the center of the play structurally, but thematically as well. It brings the action to the White House, to the Great White Father, whose help Cody had vainly promised Sitting Bull. The theme of impersonation versus authenticity is introduced by the theatrical device of "the play-within-a play," which is announced by Ned Buntline, the author of *Scouts of the Plain*. This play was the first one in which Cody impersonated himself as Buffalo Bill. The introduction in a mocking doggerel underlines the falseness and commercialism at the root of the myth of the Wild West:

> Ah, forgive me, I'm sorry, Ned Buntline's the name,
> It's me who's brought Bill Cody fame,
> Wrote twenty-seven books with him the hero
> Made 'm better known than Nero.
> And though we sold 'em cheap, one for a dime,
> The two of us was rich in no time.
> As for my soul's redemption, it came thus:
> I saw the nation profit more than us.
> For with each one o' my excitin' stories,

> Cody grew t' represent its glories.
> Also helped relieve its conscience,
> By showing pessimism's nonsense. (35)

John Lahr has pointed out that heroes of the West such as Buffalo Bill emerged at a time in our history when the language of the Great Plains was changing from that of adventure to that of profit.[20] It was a time when men like Cody who had real adventures became seduced by commercial promoters into imitating themselves in the belief that they were doing this for a higher cause: "I'm doin' what my country wants! WHAT MY BELOVED COUNTRY WANTS!" (41). In this belief, he becomes more and more convinced that Buntline is not exploiting him: "ya see, Bill (speaking to Hickok) what you fail to understand is that I'm not being false to what I was. I'm simply drawin' on what I was . . . raising it to a higher level" (42).

Cody is a man of genuine good intentions: "I think I'm doin' a lot o' good up here. Entertainin' people! Makin' 'em happy. Showin' 'em the West. Givin' 'em somethin' t' be proud of" (40).

Yet his very naiveté leads him to become an accomplice to the prostitution of his own talent, which eventually destroys the possibility of its fulfillment. It parallels the nation's good intentions, that fall victim to its refusal to look at reality. Kopit is quoted by Lahr: "This country was founded on anticipation of a dream. Yet this country refused to acknowledge that this dream was something other than what it wanted. That had to happen. But the way in which we took the country was not what we want to know. Our dream of glory was not the nightmare of destruction, of willfulness, of greed, of perjury, of murder which it became."[21]

In *Indians* Arthur Kopit shows our willingness to accept myth rather than facts by the enthusiastic reception the President gives to Buntline's absurd play. All the Indians in the Buntline play were played by actors—the chief, Uncas, by a German, the Indian maiden by an Italian—creating an even more ludicrous setting for the "real" cowboys, William Cody and Bill Hickok. The Ol' Time President is far more eager to accept this melodramatic nonsense that to learn the reality of the Indians' situation. Insofar as Buffalo Bill is willing to participate in such mythical creations, he becomes an accomplice to the Indians' destruction.

The contrast to Cody's enthusiastic participation in the play is Wild Bill Hickok, who balks at his role: "Will, stop it! A man may need money, but no man needs it this bad" (39). Hickok is so infuriated at the indignity that Buntline inflicts upon him that he kills him: "The humiliation o' havin' to impersonate my own personal self" (41).

The audience of the play-within-the-play, the Ol' Time President and the First Lady, watch Buntline's murder with fascination and complete acceptance as they do Hickok's subsequent rape of the Indian maiden. Kopit suggests an analogy to the present time, when millions of Americans were watching scenes of much greater horror, the Vietnam War, on their television screens. It has been suggested that "the meaningless violence of the Wild West stereotype fed into and encouraged an equal real-life violence."[22]

Cody's growing awareness that his positive qualities were evermore threatened by his mythic self as Buffalo Bill becomes clear at the end of this scene: "Buffalo Bill in a daze, walks to the stage and opens the curtains. 'Scouts of the Plains' drop seen. He stares at it. Pulls it down . . . He looks around in total confusion . . . Lights fade to black. Buffalo Bill is spinning dizzily in the middle" (48).

As we return to the Committee Hearing in the next scene, we are again confronted with John Grass, the Indian who still attempts to act authentically within his own tradition. The difficulty of maintaining this stance in a world where his values have become no longer viable is related to Buffalo Bill's confusion at the end of the previous scene: "The white men made our heads dizzy, and the signing was an accident" (50).

John Grass vainly protests that the Indians do not want to live like the white man: "We are happy like the Indian" (51). All he wants is "What is owed us" (51). To the senators' condescending explanation that the money is held in trust for them because they'd just spend it on liquor, he answers: "Then tell the Great Father who says he wishes us to live like white men, that when an Indian gets drunk, he is merely imitating the white men he's observed" (51).

From the discussion of imitation, the next scene, which is set in the show business world of the Wild West Show, moves on to a dramatic portrayal of impersonation. Along with Annie Oakley and the Rough Riders, Buffalo Bill announces his great show: "With alltime favorite Johnny Baker, Texas Jack and his twelve-string guitar, the Dancin' Cavanaughs, Sheriff Brad and the Dead Wood Mail Coach, Harry Philanee's Trained Prairie Dogs, The Abilene County Girls' School Trick Roping and Lasso Society, Pecos Pete and the—" (55).

Along with these tacky mementos appear his company of "authentic" Indians, who will recreate their Sun Dance, and Chief Joseph, old and barely able to walk, who "performs" his moving speech upon the occasion of his surrender to General Howard. Before the chief climbs upon an inverted tub pathetically to recreate himself, he explains his presence in this mockery of his heritage:

> William Cody came to see me. He was a nice man. With eyes that seemed . . . frightened. I . . . don't know why. He told me I was courageous and said he admired me. Then he explained all about his Wild West Show, in which the great Sitting Bull appeared, and said if I agreed to join he would have me released from prison, and see that my people received food. I asked what I could do, as I was not a very good rider or marksman. And he looked away and said, "Just repeat, twice a day, three times on Sundays, what you said that afternoon when our army caught you at the Canadian border, where you'd been heading, and where you and your people would have all been safe." So I agreed. For the benefit of my people. . . .(56)

To recreate the Sun Dance, the Indians hook the barbed ends of long leather thongs through chest harnesses and dance about the pole pretending great pain; John Grass enters and puts an end to this degrading spectacle by performing the dance authentically, hooking the thongs onto his chest muscle, until he collapses. The scene ends with Buffalo Bill cradling the bleeding, dying John Grass in his arms in a final gesture of homage to a man who had maintained his integrity.

Buffalo Bill tries once again in the tenth scene to help Sitting Bull and his tribe. He pleads with the Ol' Time President to come with him to the reservation. He finds the President riding a mechanical horse and dressed like Wild Bill Hickok: "What you want I do for 'em? Do I give 'em back their land? Do I resurrect the buffalo?" he asks (65). To Bill's plea that he could do other things, he answers: "No Cody. Other people can do other things. I . . . must do magic. Well, I can't do magic for them; it's too late" (65). Thus while thanking Buffalo Bill for his Wild West Show, "For what it's done. For this country's pride, its glory," the President appoints the Commission to whom we return in the next scene.

Once more Cody tries to explain the divergent culture of the Indian to the senators—another vain attempt at communication. He pleads: "If their way o' seein' is hard fer us t' follow, ours is just as hard fer them" (68). The senators are unwilling to respect a culture so antithetical to theirs: "The majority of 'em, ya see, don't understand how land can be owned, since they believe the land was made by the Great Spirits for the benefit of everyone. So, when we do buy land from 'em, they think it's just some kind o' temporary loan, an' figure we're kind o' foolish fer payin' good money for it, much as someone 'ud seem downright foolish t' us who paid money for the sky, say, or the ocean" (68).

Sitting Bull pretends to accept the white man's way and asks the Great Father for the means to live like white men. The senators, offended by Sitting Bull, mock his pretense of power: "You have no power, no control, and no right to any control" (73). Sitting Bull explains his pride: "If a man is the chief of a great people, and has done many great things for them, of course, he should be proud" (74).

In the English production of *Indians*, the twelfth scene was a parody of all the Western movie barroom scenes. The English critic John Russel Taylor objected to the scene in an otherwise glowing review: "It is a very long drawn-out and not particularly funny send-up of the typical film Western barroom scene with the visiting dude (in this case the President) being taken for enormous sums of money by a collection of fiercely disreputable card sharks."[23]

Kopit took the advice of the English critics. While the setting of the scene is still a stereotypical Western saloon, complete with legendary figures such as Jesse James and Billy the Kid, structurally it combines the two themes of the play—the destruction of Sitting Bull's tribe and Buffalo Bill's growing awareness of the destruction of his own authentic self. The parallels to the American involvement in Vietnam and America's loss of once authentic values become ever clearer to the audience. William Cody is looking for Wild Bill Hickok, who he believes has remained true to himself. Cody is overcome with guilt for the part he unwittingly played in the destruction of Sitting Bull, whom he genuinely loved. He can no longer find himself among the trappings of his own myth: "I'm scared. I dunno what's happenin' anymore . . . Things have gotten . . . beyond me" (77). Just as in the first scene, the shadows of the Indians invade the garish saloon, acting out Cody's words: "I see them everywhere" (77). He sees his legend as Buffalo Bill as the agent of the Indians' ultimate destruction: "I wiped out their food, ya see . . . Didn't mean to, o' course, I mean IT WASN'T MY FAULT! The railroad men needed food. They hired me t' find 'em food! Well. How was I t' know the goddam buffalo reproduced so slowly? How was I to know that. NO ONE KNEW THAT" (79).

He has become ever more involved in the Indians' fate. "The hearing was a shambles. I brought these Senators, you see. To Sitting Bull's reservation. It was a shambles" (79).

The irony of Sitting Bull's death is underlined by Cody's description of the Chief's assassination: "While the . . . wonderful gray horse I'd given him for . . . appearing in my show danced his repertory of tricks in the background since a gunshot was his cue to perform" (80).

He turns to Hickok for the answers he hopes he has, for "Hickok knows just who he is" (80). But Hickok had learned the commercial value of becoming a myth from Cody and the rationalization of such behavior as well. "Why takin' what you were and raisin' it to a higher level. Naturally for my services I get a small fee. Percentage. You get 50 percent right off the top. Of course, if at any time you aren't happy, you can leave. Take your business elsewhere," he replies cynically (81). In horror Buffalo Bill, confronted with a group of men dressed to impersonate him, shoots at these reproductions of his once authentic self. But the clones are indestructible and surround him.

The last scene shows the army officer who had slaughtered the Indians interviewed by the press. In an obvious allusion to the endless body-count reports of the Vietnam War, the Colonel reports the wiping out of the entire tribe and the loss of twenty-nine soldiers. In defense of this massacre of an entire tribe of unarmed Indians on a reservation, Kopit puts a paraphrase of Westmoreland's statement into the mouth of the commanding officer of the raiding party: "Of course it was harsh. And I don't like it any more than you. But had we shirked our responsibility, skirmishes would have gone on for years, costing our country millions, as well as untold lives. Of course innocent people have been killed. In war they always are. And of course our hearts go out to the innocent victims of this. But war is not a game. It's tough. And demands tough decisions. In the long run I believe what happened here at this reservation yesterday will be justified" (84).

Buffalo Bill justifies our policy toward the Indians, counterpointed by the recreation of the death of the Indians, to "these sentimental humanitarians who take no account of the difficulties under which this government has labored in its efforts to deal fairly with the Indians nor of the countless lives we have lost and atrocities endured at their savage hands" (90).

A symbol of the complete destruction of Indian culture is Cody's peddling of bogus Indian artifacts in the guise of helping them to help themselves. This is a concrete visualization of the destruction of the Indians themselves under the same guise of helping them which Cody has just narrated.

The circular structure of the play is completed with Buffalo Bill in his Wild West get-up on stage on his artificial horse with the display cases of the first scene back on stage.

Later discussions of the play saw the obvious parallel between *Indians* and the Vietnam War; most newspaper reviews in 1969, whether they were favorable or not, did not seem to make the connection. They dealt mainly with the historical theme of the play and the creation of a legend, but made no mention of the world outside the play.

Indians did not run longer than the 1969 theatrical season in New York. This was due mainly to the enormous cost of the production rather than to lack of interested audiences. Its sale to the movies, however, to be used as a basis for Robert Altman's film *Buffalo Bill and the Indians*, permitted Arthur Kopit once more to pursue his writing without undue financial pressure.

Chapter Twelve
The Mystery of Language
The Mediating Function of Art:
From Tragedy to Theater

When *Wings* opened at the Yale Repertory Theater in 1978, it had been almost ten years since a new Kopit play had been produced. Plays had been written; but Kopit is a meticulous craftsman who discards those works that do not meet his exacting standards. He works steadily, writing several hours each day. "I don't really see why I shouldn't be able to turn out a play every two years. It should be possible for me now," he comments. "But you see, a play has to . . . wait. It takes time."[1]

Wings sprang from an intense personal experience. In the spring of 1976 Kopit's father suffered a massive stroke which left him unable to speak. In fact, the aphasia he suffered impaired his ability to integrate most verbal processes. The playwright, in an effort to understand the isolation and terror his father was suffering, started to write about it. About that time, National Public Radio commissioned him to write a play on any subject of his choosing for performance in the "Earplay" series. Thus *Wings* was first a radio play. But Kopit, almost from the first, tried to solve the structural and technical problems of transferring it to the stage. The problems were formidable: how could the trauma of a stroke be portrayed on the stage without becoming a clinical study, without becoming so grim that the audience would turn away? He knew he would have to find another voice, not his father's, to tell his story; for he felt, "I was too close to him to hold any hope of objectivity" (xiii).[2]

Kopit solved both problems by choosing as his protagonist a female stroke victim, Emily Stilson, through whose consciousness, through whose terror of experiencing the disintegration of all she once knew, and through whose courage and spirit the audience perceives the play.

It was Emily's extraordinary valor that permitted her to explore this new, disoriented world in which she suddenly found herself in the spirit of adventure with which she had always lived. This extraordinary personality was based on a patient whom Kopit had met while visiting his father at a rehabilitation center. Like his father, this woman had had a stroke which left her aphasic. Kopit was struck with her ability to laugh at her own inability to choose appropriate words: "She had come to a station in her life from which she could perceive in what was happening something that bore the aspect of adventure, and it was through this perhaps innate capacity to perceive and appreciate adventure, and perhaps in this sense only, that she found some remaining modicum of delight, which I suspect kept her going" (1). He discovered that in the woman's youth she had been an aviatrix and wingwalker.

Wings begins with Emily Stilson's stroke, a section he entitles "Catastrophe," and progresses through "Awakening" to "Explorations." It is as Kopit characterizes it in "Notes on the production of this Play," a progress from "fragmentation to integration." The woman whom we see on the stage is "the intact inner self of Mrs. Stilson." As she comes closer to again understanding the world about her, we sometimes see her as others see her. At times toward the play's end, the inner and the outer selves merge, become integrated.

A Problem of Communication

In his choice of a stroke victim as protagonist, Kopit is able to develop two themes in *Wings* which have been present in all his works—an exploration of the nature of language and an exploration of the human condition. He sees *Wings* not as a departure but as a progression from his earlier plays: "I've always seen my plays as adventure stories and explorations of the unknown—that is, going into forbidden territory, into the Netherworld."[3] The coordinating link of the two themes is communication, in fact the difficulty of human communication. This theme can be traced in all of Arthur Kopit's plays. Jonathan's stammer in *Oh Dad, Poor Dad* is but a precursor of Emily's language problems; Emily Stilson is no more cut off from the world than are the mad women in *Chamber Music*; the gulf between Emily's world and the world of the rest of humanity is no deeper than the one between the world of the Indians and that of the Senate Committee.

Yet despite his characterization of Emily's stroke as an "Aeneas like" descent into the underworld with the hope of re-emergence always present,[4] he chose not subterranean images to describe her journey but ones of flying. Kopit prefaces *Wings* with Charles Lindbergh's words from *The Spirit of St. Louis*: "I weave in and out of the strange clouds, hidden in my tiny cockpit, submerged, alone, on the magnitude of this weird, unhuman space, venturing where man has never been, perhaps never meant to go. Am I myself a living, breathing, earth-bound body, or is this a dream of death I'm passing through? Am I alive, or am I really dead, a spirit in a spirit world. Am I actually in a plane, or have I crashed on some worldly mountain, and is this the afterlife?"[6]

Emily not only experiences her trauma in terms of flying: "OH MY GOD! CRASHING!" (24) but relates all her subsequent experiences to planes, clouds, and aviation. At the end of the play, at the moment of her acceptance of dying, at the moment of her death, she closes both the play and her life with the image of wings: "Oh my, yes, and here it goes then out . . . there I think on wings? Yes . . ." (77).

Despite the horror, the dislocation, the quality within Emily that led her in her youth to walk on the wings of airplanes permits her to view this frightening experience with more than just terror: "[With delight] What a strange adventure I'm having" (25). Thus while the world of aphasia that Emily Stilson experiences, "a world of fragments, a world without dimension, a world where time meant nothing constant, and from which there seemed no method of escape" (xv), can be defined as a metaphor for the despair of the human condition; *Wings* is not an existential play of despair. Emily's spirit and the excitement of the human mind searching for ways to escape the prison of silence lift *Wings* into a vehicle of exploring not only Emily's mind but our own as well. It is interesting to note here that the description of this world where "time meant nothing constant" evokes the last speech of *Chamber Music*: "We don't need the clocks anymore."[5]

Above all, *Wings* is a play about language, and as Kopit once said:

"Language is more than a form of communication; it's one of the ways of knowing."[6] Like the philosopher Wittgenstein, Kopit knows that only by understanding the structure and limits of language will we learn the structure and limits of thought. Thus, struggling back from an isolation that "verges on the intolerable" (viii), Emily searches for clues. "How does it work," she cries out, "What's inside that . . . makes it work?" (52). She finally confronts Amy with the unanswerable enigma of human speech:

MRS. STILSON: Where do you get names from?
AMY: I? From in here, same as you.
MRS. STILSON: Do you know how you do it?
AMY: No.
MRS. STILSON: Then how am I supposed . . . to learn?
AMY: (SOFTLY) I don't really know. (70)

If one of the functions of literature is to shock us out of "the anaesthetic grip our language maintains on our perceptions,"[7] then a stroke is the ultimate alienating device which forces us to look at language anew. "What is an arm?" Emily asks. If the basis of language's anesthetic function is the assumption that there is an unquestionable identity between the sound image made by the word "arm" and the concept of "arm," then this grip on our perceptions has been loosened for the stroke victim. Watching and contemplating Emily's struggle to make language work for her helps us to see the structure of language and the structure of our world with new eyes. Emily's desperate struggle to communicate, to express her inner feelings into words, is "the image of what is tongue-tied in all of us."[8] The play gains strength through the dynamic tension that is set up between the necessity of language to bridge the gulf between us and its inability to do it. This inability of language to set up an equivalency between feelings and words, what the Germans call *Sprachnot* ("poverty of language"), has been one of the reasons given for modern man's alienation. The stroke victim's inability to make language work for her endangers not only her knowledge of the outside world but threatens her knowledge of herself, of her personal identity as well. Who is she? Emily wonders. As she begins to be able to process some of the myriad sensations assaulting her mind, she picks up a name. "My name then—Mrs. Stilson" (27). But the victory over chaos is brief; her hold on reality precarious. Another name is processed by her injured mind, and confusion again ensues: "My name then—Mrs. Howard?" (27).

Arthur Kopit was not the first to use the damaged mind in order to illuminate our knowledge of language. The Russian formalist linguist Roman Jacobson studied aphasia in order to explore the poetic functions of language. He noted that there were two common kinds of aphasia: similarity disorder and contiguity disorder.[9] Kopit in his introduction to *Wings* noted that he modeled Emily Stilson's speech on that of two women patients—the ex-aviatrix who served as the overall model for his protagonist, who suffered from a contiguity disorder, and a young woman who suffered from similarity disorder. He described the speech of the young woman as "fluent and possessed of normal intonations, cadence and syntactic structure. . . . Nonetheless her sentences were laced with a kind of babbled jargon" (ix), as were Emily's in the beginning of the play:

MRS. STILSON: Still . . . sun moon too or . . . three times happened maybe blobbidged rubbidged uff and firded-forded me to nothing there try again. (23)

Jacobson in his study observed that in a patient suffering from similarity disorder only the syntagmatic or combinative aspect of language was operant. Thus at first their speech sounds normal. Metaphor, the poetic figure based on an analogy between a literal subject and substitute such as "The eyes are mirror of the soul," is alien to such patients. The poetic conceit they do make wide use of is metonymy, which is based on sequential association between a literal subject and its adjacent replacement. "City Hall proposes new priorities," is an example of metonymy. Here a specific building is to stand for a person, the mayor. Thus when the nurse asks Mrs. Stilson, "May I get you something?" (33) instead of saying "sweater," which she wants, she says "pillow," something else that is soft.

The older woman patient on whose character Kopit drew so much in the creation of Emily Stilson, suffering from a contiguity disorder, has lost the ability to follow the rules which organize words into higher units: "The older woman's words had no fluency, no melodic inflection, no syntactical richness. Her words emerged with difficulty and sounded like something composed for a telegram. Modifiers and conjunctions for the most part were absent" (ix). This is characteristic of Emily's speech at times when she begins to reenter the world:

DOCTOR: Mrs. Stilson, are there seven days in a week?
MRS. STILSON: . . . Seven . . . Yes.
DOCTOR: Are there five days in a week?
PAUSE.
MRS. STILSON (AFTER MUCH PONDERING): No. (35)

In order to give Emily's speech more linguistic richness, Kopit borrowed from both of the aphasic symptoms. He was, after all, writing a play, not a clinical study.

The Human Concern

Among the generally glowing reviews following the opening of *Wings* on Broadway at the end of 1978 was an attack on the play as well as on the American theater in general. Entitled "The Theatre in the Me Generation," it castigated Kopit in particular, as well as Sam Shepard among others, for not transcending "The private world of its protagonist's experience" unless "one views her flight as a Beckettian parable about the inadequacies of language or the solipsistic nature of life in general."[10] The critic clearly overlooked the real themes of *Wings*: the exploration of the nature and structure of language as the particularly human way of experiencing the world, and the stroke victim as metaphoric for the human courage which can overcome existential human isolation. It unjustly faults Kopit for turning his back on the social and public world by focusing on "the obsession with private personality and the domain of self."[11] This echoes a concern about the American theater that Arthur Kopit had expressed as a young man: "Unlike its counterparts in Sweden, France, Germany, England and Italy, it has little more than superficial relevance to the society and culture surrounding it."[12] Kopit has never explored the world of private neurosis in his plays, which have always been commentaries on the culture and society about him. In fact the suppression of the "I" has been an important concern. In a 1969 interview he noted: "When you write a play, you the author don't appear. You are impersonal. I'm very comfortable in this role."[13] Ten years later, referring to *Wings* specifically, he told the Harvard alumni magazine that he finds this his best play: "It's the first time I've been able to submerge my own voice—a playwright is a voice, after all."[14]

Since speech, language, is in the words of Kopit's Mme Rosepettle "the specialty of man" then "Our mysterious ability or inability to take command of it"[15] is far from a private concern, but perhaps the most fundamentally social concern. The critique of *Wings* exemplifies the view that in order to say something about the world, about humanity, in order to understand the connection between art and public life, only the realistic mode is viable and acceptable. This is a view that Arthur Kopit rejects for himself. "I think in blocks— images—ellipses. I'm not particularly drawn to linear progression."[16]

The character of Emily Stilson is also far from representing the "solipsistic nature of life in general." The world of the stroke victim may be the metaphor for the human condition in this cold and unfriendly planet of ours, but Emily's courage holds out hope for the "progression from fragmentation into integration." She is helped along in this journey from isolation and despair to a feeling of community and acceptance by Amy, the therapist whose love and concern permit Emily to open herself up to the world: "We're outside. Sense of distance, openness. . . . All feeling of constraint is gone" (69). Emily dies, or is about to die at the end of *Wings*, but she does not die in loneliness or despair. "Amy is still beside me" (44). The stations of Emily's journey are punctuated by the image of bright flowers, "which are the first real color we have seen," the stage directions read (35). We see flowers at the point when Emily's inner and outer worlds are beginning to come together. Later on, when her associative ability has been reactivated, it is concretized for the audience by "a vase of flowers [which] helps to signal that Mrs. Stilson's world is becoming fuller, more integrated" (52).

Kopit has been able to put on the stage both the interior workings of the mind and the human needs of the soul for love and community through the theatrical and poetic use of language. He has been able to bring together the concerns and themes that had occupied him since his undergraduate days.

Chapter Thirteen
History of
Off Broadway Theater
Origins of the Revolt

The commercial theater at the turn of the century was not very different from the commercial theater of today. Large syndicates such as the Shubert empire, then and now, controlled most of the houses and usually presented popular fare that expressed neither the literary nor the social interests of serious theater practitioners and audiences. The Off Broadway theater was, and is, a conscious revolt against this established form of theater. As far back as 1904, critics were assailing commercial theater for not responding to the social context from which it emerged. William Dean Howells wrote in *Harper's Weekly* that "English plays have to do with man as society man. . . . American plays with man as family man . . . (this is a defect of our playwrights, that it does not carry over from home to humanity)."[1] More than fifty years later, Robert Brustein, then dean of the Yale Drama School, voiced this thought: "American drama often seems to be the most mundane form of legitimate culture since eighteenth century senti- mental comedy, a form to which it has more than a little resemblance. Our serious drama is informed by a debased Freudianism, our come- dies are set in motion by man-chasing women."[2]

The nonprofit theater arose then, and still remains, as an alterna- tive to the commercial theater, as a rebuke to Broadway, as an extension not a replacement of popular theater. This theater sought serious audiences who were interested not primarily in entertain- ment, but in participating in advancing works of art. The writers, actors, and directors involved in this alternative theater were intent on expanding the artistic limits of the theater.

The theater groups began to emerge in the early 1900s around

Greenwich Village, where young intellectuals formed clubs to read aloud plays that were not being performed commercially. These groups had a strong social commitment. One of the earliest to present plays that could articulate their aims was the Progressive Stage Society whose productions stressed a radical context. Others whose interests were esthetic rather than political decided to present some plays, and thus the Washington Square Players were born. Some of these young rebels, whose announced aim was to produce American and European plays of artistic merit in direct competition with Broadway, later became famous in a variety of intellectual fields—Lawrence Langer as playwright and producer, Louis Untermeyer as poet, and Walter Lippman as columnist. With a few hundred dollars and a handful of subscribers, they opened the Bandbox Theatre at 57th Street and Third Avenue in 1915 with three one-act plays by Langer, Edward Goodman, and Maurice Maeterlinck. A short time later, the group changed its name to the Theater Guild, a prestigious organization which continues to be active and brings the best of standard repertory and more conventional new plays to the New York theater.

A decision by the Washington Square Players *not* to produce a play caused a rift, and two of the original group—Susan Glaspell and George Crambrook—left and eventually rented an old fish house at Provincetown in Cape Cod which they called the Wharf Theater. In the summer of 1916, the now-called Provincetown Players, premiered the work of a young writer, Eugene O'Neill. The group was to become famous for producing O'Neill. Its emphasis on involving the writer in the production of his work and its sponsorship of unknown dramatists embodied the spirit of Off Broadway. This medium has continued to develop the talents of the best young dramatists and has given generations of aspiring actors and directors the opportunity to perfect their craft.

Other theater groups of influence began to develop. Many followed the earlier pattern of progressing from amateur readings to professional productions. Notable among these was the Neighborhood Playhouse, which developed from a drama club at the Henry Street Settlement House. The club came to the attention of the philanthropic Lewisohn sisters, who helped it obtain a theater on Grand

Street in 1915. The group developed into a world-famous repertory company which continued performing throughout the 1920s.

In 1926, the actress Eva Le Gallienne established the Civic Repertory on 14th Street, which brought theater of great artistic merit at very low prices to the non-traditional audience. Its ambitious program featured twenty-five classics in repertory. Starring along with Le Gallienne were such greats as Nazimova and Joseph Schildkraut.

The stock market crash of 1929 sent the Off Broadway theater into a decline. Despite constant financial difficulties, the Le Gallienne group survived into the 1930s. The need for social reform and the trials of the working class motivated a new flurry of Off Broadway activities which went back to its origins in the radical plays of the early workers clubs. New theaters, under the auspices of the Workers' Drama League, the Jewish Workers' Theater, the Ukrainian Dramatic Circle, and the Workers' Laboratory Theatre, presented new plays that expressed the concerns of the audience. Clifford Odets became one of the leading spokesmen for the social unrest of the time; and a musical written and performed by members of the International Ladies Garment Workers Union—*Pins and Needles*—became an Off Broadway smash hit. The nationwide Federal Theater created paying jobs, as did the theaters run by the Works Progress Administration. Thus the Off Broadway goals were kept alive.

The left-wing Theatre of Action and the New Theatre League produced agit-prop theater alerting audiences to the danger of fascism. The only Off Broadway theater kept alive throughout World War II was the Experimental Theatre, sponsored by the Dramatist Guild and Actors' Equity, which continued to stage avant-garde plays and award scholarships.

The big spurt of growth of the Off Broadway theater came after the war. Nearly thirty new theaters opened in the first three postwar years, ushering in what can be considered Off Broadway's golden age. The noncommercial stage began to stand not only for innovation, but for distinction as well. Audiences hungered for new fare after the lean war years that had brought mostly light entertainment to the stage. New European dramatists, long cut off from American audiences, and new young American writers, who had grown up during the war, provided a supply of new material. Broadway costs were now rising so sharply that, more than ever, the commercial theater shied away from the new and untried. Off Broadway provided the answer to the countless young writers, performers, and theater technicians, as well as to the more sophisticated audience that sought an alternative to the banality of Broadway. Theater began to be played everywhere—in cafés, lofts, converted garages, basements—by groups calling themselves Associated Playwrights, New Stage, Playcrafts, Onstage, Originals Only, to name a few.

Equity, the actors' union, gave Off Broadway official recognition in 1950 by setting regulations that permitted members to appear in Off Broadway productions at a lower pay scale than for Broadway offerings. Off Broadway theaters were grouped into those of less than 199 seats and 200 to 299 seats, with the pay scale tied to the seating capacity. The geographical Off Broadway locations were defined as lying outside the area bounded by Fifth and Ninth Avenues and between 34th and 56th Streets.

Circle in the Square

Committed theater practitioners went Off Broadway as a conscious rebuke to the commercial theater. They strove to create a sense of continuity for actors, writers, and directors as well as new audiences who would share their ideals. Jose Quintero, the cofounder with Theodore Mann of the Circle in the Square, the oldest continuing Off Broadway venture, jubilantly said when they moved into their first space in 1950, "We have a place. We're not a migrant pack like Broadway producers."[3] Their dream was to create a simple partnership among director, author, and actor. The theater they opened in 1950 on Sheridan Square in Greenwich Village was in the Old Greenwich Village Inn. The group did not have a license so they could not charge admission and had to pass the hat. Their first offering, *Dark of the Moon*, used the innovative three-quarter area staging not as a way of breaking out of the proscenium box, but out of necessity. Quintero had to work with the existing nightclub stage. Yet miraculously their $7,000 stake permitted them to produce seven productions before Quintero's famous 1952 revival of Tennessee

Williams's *Summer and Smoke.* This production legitimized the efforts
of the Off Broadway professionals and is generally credited with
launching the Off Broadway boom. Although newspapers were not
reviewing Off Broadway productions, Brooks Atkinson, the respected *New York Times* drama critic, saw the production and wrote a
glowing review. "The next morning a line stretched from the box
office to the corner of the block,"[4] Theodore Mann recalls.

With *Summer and Smoke,* the two most successful aspects of Off
Broadway in the 1950s had begun—the rediscovery of plays by
well-known dramatists that had not succeeded commercially and the
discovery of new acting talent. *Summer and Smoke* not only made a hit
of a Tennessee Williams play that had failed on Broadway, but
introduced the first Off Broadway star, Geraldine Page. Off Broadway productions continued to gamble not only on plays but also on
performers whose nurturance was considered intrinsic to the noncommercial stage. Quintero commented in a 1959 interview in the
New York Post, "I have a strong resistance to Broadway stars coming
down to Off Broadway. I feel a responsibility to the new people in the
theater."[5]

After *Summer and Smoke,* the Circle in the Square's next hit was *The
Girl on the Via Flaminia.* But the beginning of success did not protect
the group from what was perceived as the harassment of the Off
Broadway theaters by various city and state agencies. Still possessing
only a cabaret license, the theater was found to be in violation of fire
laws, presenting plays to audiences that were deemed too large. The
Circle in the Square was closed in the middle of the 1954 season. *The
Girl on the Via Flaminia* was moved to a Broadway theater where it
could not sustain its Off Broadway success.

When the theater reopened in 1955, the Circle in the Square had
lost audiences to other emerging Off Broadway groups. They decided
to gamble all on a presentation of a play by the esteemed Eugene
O'Neill, whose reputation had sagged on Broadway. The spectacular
production of *The Iceman Cometh* is credited with a revival of interest in
O'Neill and the career of Jason Robards, who starred as Hickey.
Iceman ran for 556 performances, an unheard of hit for Off Broadway
of the time. Interest in both the play and the director was so great that

Mann and Quintero presented O'Neill's *Long Day's Journey into Night* on Broadway later in 1956. It established the work as the undisputed masterpiece of American drama, and the production as the definitive one. It also was a financial success, enabling the Circle in the Square to continue its work. It was the first of a number of productions by Off Broadway groups to succeed on the commercial stage, creating profits to be used to finance later experimental plays.

The success of the O'Neill production made it possible to move the group from its previous home on Sheridan Square to the theater on Bleecker Street which still bears its name. The previous home of the Amato Opera, the new Circle in the Square was a real theater with all the amenities that had been missing in the makeshift quarters on Sheridan Square. Yet the purchase of the new house exacerbated the emerging conflict between Mann, the producer, and Quintero, the director. The latter was convinced that a theater belonged to the actors, while Mann felt that responsibility and control were his, and the new house should generate income. While the Circle in the Square survives, the fruitful collaboration between the two founding fathers was not to last.

The Circle in the Square had another profound influence on the theater. It set a new standard in women's physical appearance. The success of such actresses as Geraldine Page, Salome Jens, and Colleen Dewhurst destroyed the commercial Broadway stereotype of "a small, pretty, neat girl in tennis clothes."[6] The women stars of Circle in the Square were tall, sensuous, and not conventionally pretty.

Not only the Circle in the Square, but other companies as well served as a training ground for most of Broadway's and Hollywood's successful actors. The Broadway matinee idol look was replaced by stars like George C. Scott, Peter Falk, Dustin Hoffman, and Ben Gazzara, all of whom built their reputation in Off Broadway productions.

Within a year or two of the birth of Circle in the Square, two other companies were formed which have endured to the present—the Phoenix Theater and Joseph Papp's New York Shakespeare Festival. Neither, however, has remained in the same physical location. Adaptability spelled survival for these companies.

The Phoenix Theater

Like Circle in the Square, the Phoenix Theater was created by a collaboration of artistic and business talent. While Quintero and Mann were in their twenties, the founders of the Phoenix, Norris Houghton and T. Edward Hambleton, were in their forties and had considerable experience in the theater. Houghton was a designer and Hambleton an actor and producer. The former took over the active direction, while the latter became the business manager. While Circle in the Square started with only $7,000, the Phoenix had a working capital of $25,000 and many prominent backers.

Their ambition was to create an American version of the great institutional theaters of Europe. They opened in what had been the Stuyvesant Theater on Second Avenue and 12th Street with Hume Cronyn and Jessica Tandy as their stars. In the next four seasons, their ambitious schedule included Strindberg's *Miss Julie* and *The Stronger*, Chekhov's *A Month in the Country*, Shakespeare's *Coriolanus*, Shaw's *Saint Joan*, and Brecht's *The Good Woman of Setzuan*. The cast boasted names that were to continue to light up Broadway and Hollywood—Robert Ryan, Viveca Lindfors, Uta Hagen, Alexander Scourby, Zero Mostel, Siobhan McKenna, Marcel Marceau. After four seasons that were successful on all counts but the commercial, Hambleton broke new ground by reorganizing as a nonprofit institution in order to attract money from corporations and foundations. This enabled them to continue their plan of bringing the best of repertory theater to New York with such productions as Eva Le Gallienne and Irene Worth in Schiller's *Mary Stuart* and Eli Wallach and Joan Plowright in Ionesco's *The Chairs* and *The Lesson*. One of the first Off Broadway musical hits, *Once Upon a Matress*, was presented by the Phoenix in 1958. With the help of a successful subscription drive, the Phoenix moved to East 74th Street. In eight years they presented forty-four major productions. Fine bright new talent was introduced in the new location—Frank Gilroy with *Who'll Save the Plowboy* and Arthur Kopit with *Oh Dad, Poor Dad, Mama's Hung You in the Closet and I'm Feeling So Sad*.

Throughout its history the Phoenix occupied a position somewhere between Broadway and Off Broadway in size and between commercial and art theater in audience appeal. It was the most serious of Broadway theaters and the most affluent of the Off Broadway ones. This is a position that the Circle in the Square, now under Theodore Mann's direction, has tried to emulate after its move to Broadway and 52nd Street.

Another Off Broadway company that was formed in the 1950s and never changed its emphasis was begun by Therese Hayden, Sam Wanamaker, and Anthony Quinn to give professional actors an opportunity to develop their craft further in front of live audiences. Some notable theatrical names have been associated with the group—Patricia Neal, Eli Wallach, Anne Jackson, Ben Gazzara. In its home at Riverside Drive and 103rd Street, the Equity Library Theater has continued to produce inexpensive live theater.

Off Broadway Musicals

One of the landmark productions of Off Broadway was the Mark Blitzstein version of Brecht's *The Three Penny Opera*, which opened at the Theater de Lys in March 1954. Forced to close after twelve weeks due to a previous booking at the house, it returned triumphantly fifteen months later to an unprecedented six-year run. This memorable production, which featured among others Ed Asner, Bea Arthur, and Estelle Parsons, gave New York further proof that Off Broadway theater could be artistically as well as commercially successful.

Encouraged by the tremendous popularity of *The Three Penny Opera*, other producers ventured Off Broadway revivals of musicals. The first of these, aside from the Brecht epic, to become a hit was the 1959 revival of *Leave It to Jane* at the Sheridan Square Playhouse. This production brought Patricia Brooks, Lainie Kazan, and George Segal to the attention of the critics.

The first original musical to achieve fame was the 1958 production of *Little Mary Sunshine*, which began a tradition of Off Broadway musical parodies. The most successful of all Off Broadway productions to date was the 1960 *The Fantastics*, which is still running twenty years later in a little theater on Sullivan Street. Tom Jones and Harvey Schmidt developed the play from Rostand's *Romanesques*,

little suspecting that they were to provide employment for a generation of young actors.

The Living Theater

The 1950s also saw the beginning of many new Off Broadway
groups who concentrated on revivals of classics not generally considered commercially viable. The Off Broadway audience's interest in
seeing plays by Ibsen, Strindberg, Synge, O'Casey, and Chekhov kept
small theaters busy. Among the most interesting groups, one that
showed the change in focus from the 1950s into the 1960s, is the
Living Theater of Julian Beck and his wife, Judith Malina. They were
interested in poetic theater at first and produced one of the finest Off
Broadway productions of 1948—Ezra Pound's translations of some
Japanese No plays. The police closed the theater, obstensibly because
it was a front for a brothel. It reportedly prompted Pound to comment
how else could serious theater be expected to support itself in New
York. The Becks were in continual trouble with the police because of
the controversial nature of their presentations. The 1952 production
of Jarry's *Ubu Roi* at the Cherry Lane was closed by the fire department
because clinical references to homosexuality in the play offended some
city officials, but the Becks continued to present European plays as
well as experimental American plays. Their 1959 production of *The
Connection* was a memorable theatrical event for it showed Off Broadway's turn from presenting revivals of classics to the production of
plays by unknown American writers. Its graphic and harrowing
portrayal of the lives of addicts foretold America's growing concern
over heroin addiction and the Off Broadway theater's greater involvement with current societal questions. The theater where it was
playing was closed by the authorities once again, but public interest
permitted an extended run. The Living Theater's next production,
The Brig, in 1961, prefigured concern for society's treatment not only
of prisoners but for the repressive aspects of American society as a
whole. The Becks took their theater to Europe in 1964. When they
returned in 1968, they were again in the vanguard. The climate was
changing from social activism to individual fulfillment. They introduced the concept of a peace-loving, nonviolent revolution designed

to overhaul society in *Paradise Now*. The performance was less theater than a freely structured religious service, a modern Dionysian rite in which the audience was encouraged to take part. The Becks turned from theater "to a mission that was essentially evangelical almost religious."[7] In the Beck's theater, the emerging preoccupation with the "me" generation—the search for personal fulfillment, the emphasis on the individual mystic experience—could be seen.

Joseph Papp and the Public Theater

The man, however, who has had the most profound influence on Off Broadway, as well as on New York theater in general, is Joseph Papp, the founder of the New York Shakespeare Festival. A product of the Brooklyn streets, he discovered Shakespeare in the library of Erasmus High School after he became tired of the constant gang fights of his neighborhood. He directed his first play aboard an aircraft carrier during a hitch in the navy. Included in his cast was a young dancer named Bob Fosse. After Papp's discharge, he explored the theater scene on the West Coast, directed a Little Theater group, and became stage manager of the National Company of *Death of a Salesman*, in which he doubled as an actor as well, playing the part of Biff.

1953 found Papp back in New York. He had a job as stage manager at CBS, and he began to look about for a space where he could realize his dream of bringing free Shakespeare to the people. He persuaded the minister of a small Lower East Side church to let him use its auditorium for this purpose and assembled a group of actors from a Shakespeare workshop he had already organized. He presented Shakespeare three nights a week to respectful devotees of the bard and of Off Broadway. His goal was larger audiences, however, and he was convinced that what New York needed was free Shakespeare in the city parks. In 1955, he began to look around for existing outdoor space. He found an outdoor theater that had been built by the WPA in East River Park just south of the Williamsburg Bridge. It was well equipped and apparently had been seldom used. He talked the parks department into letting him have it for the summer of 1956, and he opened *Julius Caesar* before a neighborhood crowd of over 2,000. He recalls his feelings in a later interview: "It sounded like Ebbets Field during a pre-game warm-up. Frankly, I was scared to death. . . . Most of these people had never even seen live actors before. They might stone us to death, for all I knew."[8] The audience loved it, proving Papp's belief that "the thing about Shakespeare—what made him endure—is that he transcends time and class."[9] The Lower East Side audience that came to see his production was similar to the ones that crowded the pits in Shakespeare's time.

Enboldened by his success, he was determined to enlarge his audience once again. It took him six months before he found a city official willing to let him use the six city parks to perform Shakespeare. In addition, he planned to use a mobile stage mounted on a van to bring Shakespeare into the city streets. He finally persuaded the city to permit him to use the parks, give him some parks department employees to maintain his theaters, and to provide folding chairs and police protection. He had everything but money to stage three plays with revolving casts of four hundred actors at six locations for a total of forty-two performances. He was able to raise $30,000. When *Romeo and Juliet* opened in Central Park in the summer of 1957, it received rave reviews. Walter Kerr of the *New York Herald-Tribune* called it "in many respects the best *Romeo and Juliet* I have ever seen."[10] It was a most successful season for the group, which was now officially called the New York Shakespeare Festival. In addition to *Romeo and Juliet*, they also presented *Macbeth* and *Two Gentlemen of Verona* to excellent reviews.

By the end of the summer, Papp had decided to concentrate on Central Park, where the audiences had been the largest and the most receptive. In January 1958, he appealed to the city council directly for funds. He was not successful, but he did get a financial grant from Actor's Equity and a substantial amount from a fund raising concert held at Carnegie Hall with music based on Shakespeare's themes.

He devoted his full time to the Shakespeare Festival, having lost his TV job for refusing to testify about Communist activities on the West Coast. In the summer of 1959, he became embroiled in a bitter fight with Parks Commissioner Robert Moses, who wanted him to charge admission to the performances in order to defray expenses. When Papp refused, Moses leveled an ultimatum—"Charge admission—or get out." The press was most supportive of this champion of free theater, especially after an anonymous letter was passed around re-hashing his pleading the Fifth Amendment in front of the House Un-American Activities Committee, and declaring him unfit to run a theater. Public opinion was all on his side, and he was able to continue the performances. The publicity engendered by the affair brought about contributions that were sorely needed.

By the summer of 1962, he was able to build a permanent summer home for the festival in Central Park—the Delacorte Theater. When he went to England in 1964, he was ready to expand his theatrical vision. He had always understood that producing Shakespeare would be only a beginning of his dream of theater for the people. When he saw how the Royal Shakespeare Company mixed modern plays with Shakespeare in their repertory, he visualized how his own company might grow.

He began searching for a winter theater. The festival had a financial hit on its hands for the first time in the musical version of *Two Gentlemen from Verona*, which was put on a paying basis after its free summer stint in Central Park. In 1967, Papp founded the Public Theater after he had bought the old Astor Library on Lafayette Street for about half a million dollars. He set about transforming this huge space into five different theaters. He had to abandon his free admission policy, but continues to this day to make the tickets affordable.

In 1971, he persuaded Mayor Lindsay to purchase the now re-furbished theater and lease it back to the Shakespeare Festival for one dollar a year. He continued to bring not only theater but also dance to the Public Theater. Papp supported his commitment to new drama-tists by the ingenious device of moving plays that became hits at the Public Theater to Broadway, thus subsidizing new experimental productions. Plays that were first produced by Papp at the Public Theater and then became commercial successes were, among others, *Hair*, *That Championship Season*, and *A Chorus Line*.

In 1973, the board of Lincoln Center asked the Public Theater to take over the management of the two theaters at Lincoln Center—the Beaumont and the smaller Mitzi Newhouse Theater. This made Joe Papp into a cultural czar of New York, controlling the five theaters at the Public Theater, the summer productions, as well as several Broadway productions that had been brought up from the Public.

He decided to bring new American plays to the stage of the Beaumont and experimental Shakespeare productions to the smaller theater. Papp had by now attracted a group of new writers whose work he was determined to bring to the larger audiences at the Beaumont. Foremost among them was David Rabe, whose *In the Boom Boom Room* opened the Beaumont season. He ran into problems with the subscription audience at the Beaumont who were offended and bored by many of the new plays.

He decided, after two seasons, to emphasize new productions of established plays. The Beaumont's *Cherry Orchard*, directed by Andre Serbin, and Richard Foreman's stylized *Three Penny Opera* were memorable and successful. But the financial problems of the Shakespeare Festival were exacerbated by the enormous expense of running the Lincoln Center Theaters. Papp resigned from the directorship of the Beaumont, citing not only financial problems but that "he didn't like the essentially middle class audiences."[11] His main commitment remains to young playwrights and to unorthodox interpretations of the classics. Despite his enormous success, he continues to be beset by money problems, which forced him to curtail the 1980 summer season at the Delacorte to one offering—*The Pirates of Penzance*. This was the first season since Papp had begun producing that New York did not have free Shakespeare.

Papp has continued to attract audiences to the Public Theater as well as actors and actresses who have become commercial successes after their start with him. For the 1980—81 season, he formed a repertory company starring some of his now phenomenally successful protégés—Jill Clayburgh, Meryl Streep, Robert de Niro, and Raul Julia. They agreed to work for six months at the Equity scale salary of $225 per week. He presented as part of the season a new Sam Shepard play. Papp is "greatly concerned about writers making a living. They can't make a living Off Broadway or in Regional Theater."[12] It is the loyalty he engenders in writers and performers that has made possible the Public Theater. "Millions of people have been drawn to the theater by his productions, many for the first time. And the theater artists who enjoy his sponsorship are finding an open forum for serious expression that is practically unequalled anywhere in the country."[13] Papp's accomplishments have brought an expression of esteem from the most powerful force in commercial theater, Bernard Jacobs, president of the Shubert Organization: "It would have been almost impossible to have this renaissance in the theater without Papp."[14]

The Search for New Outlets in the 1960s

The bridge from the primarily revival-oriented 1950s to the increasingly more political 1960s was provided by a new phenomenon, the Off Broadway revue, which became popular in the early 1960s. Much of the young talent arrived from Chicago, from a little club calling itself The Second City—Mike Nichols, Elaine May, Barbara Harris, Alan Arkin. Working in the tradition of the European cabaret, such revues as *Alarum and Excursions* (1962) began to articulate the rising anxiety about the Vietnam conflict, while in the 1963 *The Living Premise* young black artists like Geoffrey Cambridge and Diana Sands began to bring black issues to the forefront.

As Off Broadway became more and more successful, it became more cautious, and young writers began to look for new outlets that would permit them to go the limits of their material.[15] As in the early 1950s, there was again an attempt to simplify the partnership between writer and author and director, and to remain small and untempted by commercialism. Robert Brustein charged that Off Broadway, perhaps due to its success, became displaced upwards into a position similar to the Broadway one it had originally reacted against. Off Broadway figures were being made into media personalities—Tom O'Horgan, Julian Beck, and Richard Schechner were being promoted the same way as Joshua Logan, William Inge, and Ethel Merman. "Artistic activity becomes another form of advertising which arbitrates its standards and evaluates it like any other product for its impact upon the consumer rather than any intrinsic merit."[16]

Off-Off Broadway

A movement that was to be known as Off-Off Broadway began to evolve from coffee houses of the Village. What started as poetry readings grew into drama and mini-productions. The first real impresario of this type was Joe Cino in his coffee house on Cornelia Street, but the most prolific and longest-lasting has been Ellen Stewart's Cafe La Mama, which, since its inception in 1960, has been dedicated to new writers. Among the playwrights who were given an opportunity to have their works performed were Claude Van Italie, Julie Bovasso, Lanford Wilson, and Sam Shepard.

The Off-Off Broadway theater began to become more and more of a force in the mid-1960s, as it developed into an artistic alternative, as well as a means of political expression against the war in Vietnam and what was perceived to be an ever-increasing atmosphere of repression. There were now confrontations in American society, not only in the antiwar movement but with the law regarding erotic plays. Writers of the mid-1960s began to expand the limits of what could be shown on the stage in plays dealing with sexual deviation such as Langford Wilson's *The Madness of Lady Bright* and *Balm in Gilead* and Rochelle Owen's *Futz*, a tale of sodomy and of a rural innocent's passion for his sow. The theater's run-in with the law usually ended with a judicial rout of censorship. "The volume of dissent had managed to blow open the doors and windows of the American theatre."[17]

One of the most memorable productions of the 1960s and one of the monuments of the antiwar movement was the 1966 Village Gate production of Barbara Garson's *MacBird*. Its significance rests not on its artistic merits, which were slight, but on its "authority of history [which] made it possible for the performing arts to use the freedoms generated under the Bill of Rights."[18] Its savage attack on the Johnsons and the Kennedys and the whole structure of American politics in the guise of a parody of a Shakespeare play was true agit-prop against our role in Vietnam.

Besides the open exploration of the sexually deviant and the political conformists, Off-Off Broadway in the 1960s also turned to what Little calls the "personality-centered"[19] workshop of such theater practitioners as Richard Schechner (Performance Group), Richard Foreman (Ontological-Hysterical Theater), Andre Gregory (Manhattan Project), John Vaccaro (Theater of the Ridiculous), and Joseph Chaikin (Open Theatre). Each of these groups was used to express the theatrical vision of a director and each expanded the possibilities of theater. Schechner, the most articulate spokesman of a particular theatrical vision, stated in a December 13, 1970, *New York Times* interview: "Theater is an unliterary art here and now experience. Its finest expressions are immediate, gestural, involved, inclusive and participatory."

The Ontological-Hysterical Theater of Foreman almost banished the playwright in its attempt to explore objective reality in a kind of highly sophisticated game built around the simple arrangement of furniture or props.

Joseph Chaikin's Open Theatre lasted from 1963 to 1973 with the stated purpose "to make viable the human situation at a time when things could be better."[20] He wanted to teach actors an eclectic technique drawn from various theoreticians from Stanislavski to Julian Beck. The group was dedicated to collective efforts of writers, actors, and directors to invent new theatrical metaphors. The two plays the Open Theatre produced in the mid-1960s, *America Hurrah* and *Viet Rock*, stand as milestones of the group's and Off-Off Broadway's achievement. While the former was written by Claude Van Italie and the latter by Megan Terry, the plays seem to be, according to Kauffmann, inseparable from the entity of the Open Theatre.[21] *America Hurrah* was Van Italie's vision of a mechanized, dehumanized, and brutalized America. The author provided the group with the lines and the subjects he wanted to treat, but the company created the production with its dancelike movements, its choruslike commentary, its lizzard props and costumes. The third act is performed by gigantic papier-mâché figures against a background of recorded cries. The other two acts deal with such aspects of contemporary American life as job interviews and TV ads, emphasizing the impersonal and banal aspects of our lives.

Megan Terry's *Viet Rock* was less propanganda against the Vietnam War than "a rhapsody and imaginative theatre exercise on the idea of all war, using performers and words and music as an abstract painter uses lights, sounds and objects."[22] While Terry supplied a working script, as had Van Italie for *America Hurrah*, Chaikin used every theatrical effect, particularly the bodies and voices of the performers, to create a kaleidoscopic view of the theme of war. The actors contributed not only their physical resources but their imaginative ones as well to the script through improvisation. The last production of the Open Theatre was the 1973 *Night Walk*, a joint effort by Van

Italie, Terry, and Shepard. According to the critics, it contained little coherent dialogue. The group's insistence on collective decisions may, according to Robert Brustein, have resulted in the playwright's lines being voted down by the actors. This focus on participatory democracy prevented the Open Theater from subordinating individual concerns to what they perceive to be the "autocracy" of a single mind.

The groups that began in the 1960s and actively continue to support the cause of new and often controversial theater are the Chelsea Theater begun at the St. Peter's Church in 1965 and the American Place Theater, started at St. Clement's Church in 1964. The Chelsea group gave two leading black playwrights their start— Ed Bullin (*Black Quartet*) and LeRoi Jones (*Slaveship*). The success of Off Broadway black theater focused attention on the black experience and made possible the formation in 1967 of the Negro Ensemble Company. The American Place Theatre produced such memorable plays as Robert Lowell's *The Old Glory* and William Alfred's *Hogan's Goat*. Their continued concern for bringing inexperienced talent to the theater can be seen by their recent involvement in producing new plays by women writers.

Several new groups begun in the 1970s successfully continue to carry out their missions. The Roundabout Theater has devoted itself to presenting the best European and American plays as well as giving new productions of less often performed works of such noted playwrights as Shaw and Ibsen. Both the Circle Repertory and the Manhattan Theater Club have given audiences the opportunity of seeing works of new writers and, at the same time, the more serious work of writers who have been successful in more commercially viable ventures. Lynne Meadow, the artistic director of the Manhattan Theater Club, expressed the spirit that has characterized Off Broadway from its inception: "The creative spirit is indomitable. If it is no longer possible to do innovative work Off Broadway, then it will be done on Off Off Broadway, and if that becomes impossible an Off Off Off Broadway will spring up."[23]

Notes and References

References without page numbers come from the clipping files of the New York Public Library's theater archives at Lincoln Center.

Chapter One

1. Marilyn Stasio, "An Outlaw Comes Home," *After Dark*, January 1980, p. 58.
2. Sam Shepard, "Autobiography," *News of the American Place Theatre*, 3, no. 3 (April 1971).
3. Kenneth Chubb, "Metaphors, Mad Dogs and Old Time Cowboys," *Theatre Quarterly* 17 (August 1974):5.
4. Sam Shepard, "Visualization, Language and The Inner Library," *Drama Review*, 21, no. 4 (December 1977).
5. Claude Levi-Strauss, *Myth and Meaning* (New York: Schocken Books, 1979) p. 20.
6. Sam Shepard, *Angel City & Other Plays* (New York: Urizen Books, 1978) p. 13.
7. George Stambolian, "Shepard's *Mad Dog Blues*: A Trip Through Popular Culture," *Journal of Popular Culture* 7 (Spring 1974): p. 776−86.
8. Shepard, "Visualization," p. 53.
9. Ibid., p. 52.
10. Ibid., p. 53.
11. Ibid.
12. Ibid., p. 50.
13. Richard Schechner, *Contemporary Dramatists* (New York: St. Martin's Press, 1973), p. 697.
14. Sam Shepard, in an unpublished letter to the author dated 1/11/80.
15. Bertolt Brecht, *The Threepenny Opera* (New York, 1966), p. 75.
16. Shepard "Visualization, Language and the Inner Library," p. 55.
17. Leslie Fiedler, *Love and Death in the American Novel* (Cleveland and New York: Meridian Books, 1960), p. xx.
18. Stasio, p. 60.

Chapter Two

1. Chubb, "Metaphors", p. 60.

2. Ibid.

3. In an unpublished letter to the author dated 12/7/79.

4. Chubb, "Metaphors," p. 8.

5. In an interview in the *New York Tribune*, 2/6/66.

6. Chubb, "Metaphors," p. 5.

7. Ibid., p. 6.

8. Ibid., p. 8.

9. Shepard, "Visualization," p. 57.

10. Ibid., p. 56.

11. Chubb, "Metaphors," p. 6.

12. Ibid., p. 8.

13. C. W. Bigsby et al., "Theatre Checklist No. 3, Sam Shepard," *Theatrefacts*, August 1974, p. 4.

14. Ibid., p. 4.

15. Ibid.

16. Richard A. Davis, " 'Get Up Outa' Your Homemade Beds': The Plays of Sam Shepard," *Players* 47 (October/November 1971):16.

17. Robert Shayon, in *Saturday Review*, April 9, 1966, p. 52.

18. Davis, p. 14.

19. Chubb, "Metaphors," p. 9.

20. Bigsby, p. 4.

21. Robert Schroeder, ed., *The Underground Theatre* (New York, 1968), p. 80.

22. Chubb, "Metaphors," p. 9.

23. Ibid.

24. Schroeder, p. vii.

25. Unsigned review in the *New Yorker*, May 11, 1968, p. 91.

26. Shepard "Visualization," p. 58.

27. Ibid.

28. Quoted by Ren Frutkin in "Sam Shepard: Paired Existence Meets the Monster," *Yale Theatre*, Summer 1969, p. 28.

29. Bigsby, p. 6.

30. Sam Shepard, "Time," *Theatre*, Spring 1978, p. 10.

31. Kenneth Chubb, "Fruitful Difficulties of Directing Shepard," *Theatre Quarterly*, August 1974, p. 19

32. Ibid.

33. Shepard, "Visualization," p. 50.

34. Frutkin, p. 25.

35. Chubb, "Fruitful Difficulties," p. 20.

36. Robert Brustein, *The Culture Watch* (New York, 1975), p. 82.

37. Quoted in Brustein, *Culture Watch*, p. 83.

38. Mel Gussow, "Sam Shepard, Writer on the Way Up," *New York Times*, November 12, 1964.

Chapter Three

1. Page references in the text are to *Operation Sidewinder*, in *The Great American Life-Show*, eds. John Laker and Jonathan Price (New York, 1974).

Chapter Four

1. Chubb, "Metaphors," p. 11.

2. Ibid., p. 12.

3. Michael VerMeulen, "Sam Shepard: Yes, Yes, Yes," *Esquire*. February 1980, p. 80.

4. Chubb, "Metaphors," p. 10.

5. Ibid.

6. Ibid.

7. Ibid., p. 5.

8. Ibid., p. 3.

9. Shepard, "Autobiography."

10. Chubb, "Metaphors," p. 5.

11. Ibid.

12. Ibid., p. 12.

13. Sam Shepard, from an unpublished letter to the author dated 12/7/79.

14. Bertolt Brecht, *Jungle of Cities* (New York, 1966), p. 12. Page references to this edition are in the text.

15. Frederick Ewen, *Bertolt Brecht* (New York, 1967), p. 118.

16. Quoted in Karl Heinz Schoeps, *Bertolt Brecht* (New York: Ungar, 1977), p. 91.

17. Martin Esslin, *Brecht* (New York: Doubleday, 1961), p. 80.

18. Walter Weideli, *The Art of Bertolt Bercht* (New York: New York University Press, 1963), p. 53.

19. Stéphane Mallarmé, *Poems*, tr. Roger Fry (New York: New Directions, 1951), p. 51.

20. Ted Hughes, "A Childish Prank," in his *Crow* (New York: Harper and Row, 1971), p. 7.

21. Chubb, "Metaphors," p. 11.

132   SHEPARD, KOPIT, AND THE OFF BROADWAY THEATER

22. Shepard, "Visualization," p. 56.
23. All page references in the text are to *The Tooth of Crime* (New York: Grove Press, 1974).
24. Chubb, "Fruitful Difficulties," p. 21.
25. Ibid., p. 12.
26. Linda Winters, *Chicago Tribune*, January 6, 1974.
27. From an unpublished letter to the author dated 1/11/80.

Chapter Five

1. Sam Shepard, *Action*, in *Angel City, Curse of the Starving Class and Other Plays* (New York, 1978). Page references in the text.
2. From an unpublished letter to the author dated December 7, 1979.
3. Chubb, "Metaphors," p. 13.
4. Chubb, "Fruitful Difficulties," p. 22.
5. Chubb, "Metaphors," p. 14.
6. Shepard, "Visualization," p. 52.
7. VerMeulen, "Sam Shepard," p. 80.
8. Carol Rosen, "Sam Shepard's Angel City: A Movie for the Stage," *Modern Drama* 22 (Spring 1979):40.
9. Irene Oppenheim and Victoria Ipscio, "The Most Promising Playwright in America Today Is Sam Shepard," *Village Voice*, October 23, 1975, pp. 81–82.
10. Ibid.
11. Shepard, *Angel City*, p. 21.
12. Sam Shepard, *Suicide in B Flat* (New York, 1979). Page references in the text.
13. Chubb, "Metaphors, " p. 3.
14. Ibid., p. 16.
15. Ross Wetzstein, *Village Voice*, June 7, 1977.
16. Shepard, *Angel City*, p. 64. Subsequent page references in the text.
17. Sam Shepard, *Seduced* (New York, 1979). Page references in the text.
18. William Kleb, "Sam Shepard's *Inacoma* at the Magic Theatre," *Theatre* 9 (Fall 1977):60.

Chapter Six

1. VerMeulen, "Sam Shepard," p. 81.
2. Ibid.
3. From an unpublished letter to the author dated 12/7/79.

4. Sam Shepard, *Buried Child* (New York, 1979). Page references are in the text.

5. Howard Clurman, in the *Nation*, December 2, 1978.

Chapter Seven

1. Eileen Blumenthal, "Chaiken and Shepard Speak in Tongues," *Village Voice*, November 26, 1979, p. 103.

2. Terence Hawkes, *Structuralism and Semiotics* (Berkeley and Los Angeles, 1977), p. 20.

3. From an unpublished letter to the author dated 12/7/79.

4. Hawkes, p. 27.

5. From an unpublished letter to the author dated 1/11/80.

6. Blumenthal, p. 108.

7. Ibid.

8. Ibid.

9. Ibid.

10. Ibid., p. 103.

11. Ibid.

12. Ibid., p. 109.

Chapter Eight

1. Judith Parker, "A Play Has to Breathe," *Harvard Magazine*, March-April 1979, p. 91.

2. Whitney Bolton, in the *Morning Telegraph*, March 3, 1961.

3. Parker, p. 91.

4. Melinda Jo Guttman, interview, *Soho News*, February 2, 1979.

5. Arthur Kopit, *The Day the Whores Came Out to Play Tennis and Other Plays* (New York, 1965), p. ix.

6. Ibid.

7. Ibid.

8. Gaynor Braddish, in the Introduction to *Oh, Dad, Poor Dad, Mamma's Hung You in the Closet and I'm Feelin' So Sad* (New York, 1960), p. 10. This will be referred to as *Oh Dad, Poor Dad* in subsequent notes and in the text.

9. Ibid., p. 11.

10. Ibid.

11. Arthur Kopit, *"Sing to Me Through Open Windows,"* in *The Day the Whores Came Out to Play Tennis and Other Plays* (New York, 1965). Page references in the text.

12. Braddish, p. 11.
13. Quoted by John Crosby in the *New York Herald Tribune*, May 20, 1962.
14. Quoted by Irving Drutman in the *New York Herald Tribune*, March 7, 1965.
15. Guttman interview.
16. Quoted by Meryle Secrest in the *Washington Post*, April 20. 1969.
17. Ibid.
18. Hawkes, p. 71.
19. Secrest interview.
20. Hawkes, p. 72.
21. Arthur Kopit, "The Vital Matter of Environment," *Theater Arts*, April, 1961, p. 36.

Chapter Nine

1. George Wellworth, *The Theater of Protest and Paradox* (New York, 1964).
2. *Variety*, March 25, 1964.
3. Martin Esslin, *The Theatre of the Absurd* (Garden City, N.Y., 1969), p. 270.
4. Robert Corrigan, "The Theatre in Search of a Fix," in *Theatre in the Twentieth Century* (New York: Grove Press, 1963), p. 12.
5. Ibid., p. 11.
6. Ibid., p. 13.
7. Ibid.
8. Arthur Kopit, *Oh Dad, Poor Dad* (New York, 1960). Page references in the text.
9. Harvard interview, p. 92.
10. Quoted by Martin Esslin in "The Theatre of the Absurd," in *Theatre in the Twentieth Century*, p. 231.
11. Esslin, *Theatre in the Twentieth Century*, p. 35.
12. Zoltan Szilassy, "Yankee Burlesque or Metaphysical Farce?" *Hungarian Studies in English* 11 (Debrecen 1977):143.
13. Ibid., p. 146.
14. Ibid.
15. George Oppenheimer, review in *Newsday*, March 7, 1962.

Chapter Ten

1. Arthur Kopit, *The Day the Whores Came Out to Play Tennis* (New York, 1965). Page references in the text.

2. Anne Murch, "Genet-Triana-Kopit: Ritual as 'Danse Macabre,'" *Modern Drama* 15 (March 1973):369—81.

3. Ibid., p. 376.

4. D. L. Rinear, *"The Day the Whores Came Out to Play Tennis*: Kopit's Debt to Chekhov," *Today's Speech*, Spring 1974, pp. 19—23.

5. Ibid.

Chapter Eleven

1. John Lahr, "Arthur Kopit's *Indians*: Dramatizing National Amnesia," *Up Against the Fourth Wall* (New York, 1969) p. 154.

2. Ibid.

3. Parker, p. 92.

4. Lahr, p. 157.

5. Ibid., p. 148.

6. Ibid., p. 153.

7. Levi-Strauss, p. 43.

8. Bruce Curtis, "The Use and Abuse of the Past in American Studies: Arthur Kopit's *Indians*, A Case Study," *American Examiner* 1 (1973):5.

9. Quoted in Robert Asahiha, "The Basic Training of American Playwrights: Theater and the Vietnam War," *Theatre* (Spring 1978), p. 33.

10. Harvard interview, p. 92.

11. Lewis Funke, "Origins of *Indians* as Recalled by Kopit," *New York Times*, October 15, 1969.

12. Curtis, p. 5.

13. Vera Jiji, *"Indians*: A Mosaic of Memories and Methodologies," Players 47 (1972):230.

14. Carol Billman, "Illusion of Grandeur, Altman, Kopit and the Legends of the Wild West," *Literature/Film Quarterly* 6 (Summer 1978):253.

15. Ibid., p. 256.

16. Arthur Kopit, *Indians* (New York, 1969). Page references in text.

17. J. B. Jones, "Impersonation and Authenticity: The Theatre as Metaphor in Kopit's *Indians*," *Quarterly Journal of Speech*, 59 (1973):446.

18. Jiji, p. 235

19. Barbara Hurrell, "Oh, Say, Can You See," *American Examiner* 1 (1973):1—3.

20. Lahr, p. 140.

21. Ibid., p. 138.

22. Jiji, p. 233.

23. Russell Taylor, "Kopit Goes West," *Plays and Players* 15 (1968): 10.

Chapter Twelve

1. Parker, p. 91.
2. Arthur Kopit, *Wings* (New York, 1978). Page references in text.
3. Guttman interview.
4. Interview with Tom Topor, *New York Post*, February 1, 1979.
5. Arthur Kopit, *Chamber Music* (New York, 1965) p. 38.
6. Richard Eder, in the *New York Times*, June 22, 1978.
7. Hawkes, p. 70.
8. Eder.
9. Roman Jacobson and Morris Halle, *Fundamentals of Language* (The Hague: Mouton, 1956), pp. 69–76. Quoted by Hawkes, p. 76.
10. Roger Copeland, "The Theatre in the Me Generation," *New York Times*, June 3, 1979.
11. Ibid.
12. Kopit, "Vital Matter of Environment," p. 36.
13. Secrest interview.
14. Parker, p. 91.
15. Guttman interview.
16. Parker, p. 92.

Chapter Thirteen

1. Morris Freedman, *American Drama in Social Context* (Carbondale, Ill., 1971), p. 101.
2. Ibid., p. 12.
3. Stuart Little, *Off Broadway: The Prophetic Theater* (New York, 1972), p. 43.
4. Ralph Tyler, "Off Broadway Marks an Anniversary," *New York Times*, Arts and Leisure Section, September 28, 1980.
5. Little, p. 64. Quoting from a 1959 *New York Post* interview with Jose Quintero.
6. Little, p. 56.
7. Robert Brustein, *The Third Theatre* (New York, 1970), p. 3.
8. Joseph Papp, in the *New Yorker*, August 31, 1957.
9. Ibid.
10. Ibid.
11. Joseph Papp, in *Variety*, June 15, 1977.
12. Tom McMorrow, "Theatre for All Seasons," *New York Theatre Review* 7 (October 1978).
13. Ibid.

14. Ibid.
15. Brustein, *Culture Watch*, p. 4.
16. Ibid.
17. Ibid., p. 36.
18. Ibid.
19. Little, p. 192.
20. Brustein, *Third Theatre*, p. 40.
21. Stanley Kauffmann, *Persons of the Drama* (New York, 1976), p. 20.
22. Ibid., p. 30.
23. Tyler.

Selected Bibliography

PRIMARY SOURCES

Kopit, Arthur. *The Day the Whores Came Out to Play Tennis and Other Plays.* New York: Hill and Wang, 1965.

———. *Indians.* New York: Hill and Wang, 1969.

———. *Oh Dad, Poor Dad, Mamma's Hung You in the Closet and I'm Feeling So Sad.* New York: Hill and Wang, 1960.

———. "The Vital Matter of Environment." *Theater Arts.* April 1961. Discusses the relation between the artist and his cultural millieu.

———. *Wings.* New York: Hill and Wang, 1978.

Shepard, Sam. [Volumes of plays in alphabetical order are followed by miscellaneous works.] *Angel City, Curse of the Starving Class and Other Plays.* New York: Urizen Books, 1978. Collection also contains *Killer's Head, Action, Mad Dog Blues, Cowboy Mouth, the Rock Garden,* and *Cowboys No. 2.*

———. *Buried Child, Seduced, Suicide in B Flat.* New York: Urizen Books, 1979.

———. *Five Plays.* Indianapolis: Bobbs-Merrill, 1969. Contains *Chicago, Icarus's Mother, Fourteen Hundred Thousand, Red Cross, Melodrama Play.*

———. *Mad Dog Blues and Other Plays.* Indianapolis: Bobbs-Merrill, 1971. Contains *Cowboys No. 2, Cowboy Mouth.*

———. *Operation Sidewinder.* Indianapolis: Bobbs-Merrill, 1970. Also published in *The Great American Life-Show.* Edited by John Laker and Jonathan Price. New York: Bantam Books, 1974.

———. *Red Cross.* In *The New Underground Theater.* Edited by Robert Schroeder. New York: Bantam Books, 1968.

———. *Tooth of Crime and Geography of a Horse Dreamer.* New York: Grove Press, 1974.

———. *Unseen Hand and Other Plays.* Indianapolis: Bobbs-Merrill, 1971. Contains *4-H Club, Forensic and the Navigators, The Holy Ghostly, Shaved Splits, Back Bog Beast Bait.*

———. *Zabriskie Point.* New York: Simon and Schuster, 1972.

———. "Autobiography." *News of the American Place Theatre*, no. 3

(April 1971). Shepard's attempt to convince the earnest playgoer of his contempt for intellectualism and his overriding interest in rock, sex, and drugs.

_____. "Time." *Theater*, Spring 1978.

_____. "Visualization, Language and The Inner Library." *Drama Review* 21 (December 1977). Shepard's thoughts on the writing of plays.

_____. *Hawk Moon*. Los Angeles: Black Sparrow Press, 1973. Short stories and poems.

SECONDARY SOURCES

Asahiha, Robert. "The Basic Training of American Playwrights: Theater and the Vietnam War." *Theater*, Spring 1978, pp. 30–35. Discusses relation of *Indians* to the war.

Bigsby, C. W., et al. "Theatre Checklist No. 3, Sam Shepard." *Theatrefacts*, August 1974. Valuable information on all Shepard plays from 1964 to 1974.

Billman, Carol. "Illusions of Grandeur, Altman, Kopit, and the Legends of the Wild West." *Literature/Film Quarterly* 6 (Summer 1978): 253–61. Comparison of Robert Altman's film version of *Indians* to the play.

Blumenthal, Eileen. "Chaiken and Shepard Speak in Tongues." *Village Voice*, November 26, 1979. Interview with both delineating their collaboration.

Bolton, Whitney. *Morning Telegraph*, March 3, 1961. Review of *Oh Dad, Poor Dad, Mamma's Hung You in the Closet and I'm Feelin' So Sad*.

Brecht, Bertolt. *Jungle of Cities*. New York: Grove Press, 1966.

_____. *The Threepenny Opera*. New York: Grove Press, 1966

Brustein, Robert. *The Culture Watch: Essays on Theatre and Society, 1969–1974*. New York: Alfred A. Knopf, 1975. Collection of essays looking at theater as a means of learning about society.

_____. *The Third Theatre*. New York: Simon & Schuster, 1970. Collection of pieces dealing with theater primarily in New York.

Chubb, Kenneth. "Fruitful Difficulties of Directing Shepard." *Theatre Quarterly*, August 1974, pp. 17–23. The British director discusses Shepard's rejection of conventional dramatic structure.

_____. "Metaphors, Mad Dogs and Old Time Cowboys." *Theatre Quarterly*

17 (August 1974): 3 – 16. The first in-depth interview with Shepard by a British director.

Clurman, Howard. Review of *Buried Child*. *Nation*, December 2, 1978.

Copeland, Roger. "The Theatre in the Me Generation." *New York Times*, June 3, 1979. A plea for more involved, engaged theater.

Curtis, Bruce. "The Use and Abuse of the Past in American Studies: Arthur Kopit's Indians, A Case Study." *American Examiner* 1, no. 4 (1973). The historian approves of Kopit's use of the past.

Davis, Richard A. " 'Get Up Outa' Your Homemade Beds': The Plays of Sam Shepard." *Players* 47 (October-December 1971). The plays up to *Operation Sidewinder*. Interpretations of *Icarus's Mother* and *Operation Sidewinder* are of merit.

Esslin, Martin. *The Theatre of the Absurd*. Garden City, New York: Anchor Books, 1969. Definitive discussion of the nature of the theater of the absurd.

Ewen, Frederick. *Bertolt Brecht*. New York: Citadel Press, 1967. In-depth discussion of Brecht's life and works.

Freedmann, Morris. *American Drama in Social Context*. Carbondale: Southern Illinois University Press, 1971. The social origins of the theater.

Frutkin, Ren. "Sam Shepard: Paired Existence Meets the Monster." *Yale Theatre*, no. 2 (Summer 1969). Close readings of some of Shepard's early plays: *Red Cross*, *Cowboys No. 2*.

Funke, Lewis. "Origins of *Indians* as Recalled by Kopit." *New York Times*, October 15, 1969. Interview during New York run of *Indians*.

Greenberger, Howard. *The Off Broadway Experience*. Englewood Cliffs, New Jersey: Prentice-Hall, 1971. History of the alternative theater.

Gussow, Mel. "Sam Shepard, Writer on the Way Up." *New York Times*, November 12, 1964. The reviewer recognized Shepard's talents early in his career.

Guttman, Melinda Jo. *Soho News*, February 2, 1979. During the New York run of *Wings*, Kopit discusses the unity of his vision.

Hawkes, Terence. *Structuralism and Semiotics*. Berkeley and Los Angeles: University of California Press, 1977. Superb presentation of the fundamentals of structuralism and semiotics.

Hurrell, Barbara. "Oh, Say, Can You See." *American Examiner* 1 (1973). Visual metaphors in *Indians*.

Jiji, Vera. "*Indians*: A Mosaic of Memories and Methodologies." *Players* 47 (1972). Discussion of play's structure.

Jones, J. B. "Impersonation and Authenticity: The Theatre as Metaphor in Kopit's *Indians*." *Quarterly Journal of Speech* 59 (1973). Valuable scene by scene interpretation.

Kauffmann, Stanley. *Persons of the Drama.* New York: Harper & Row, 1976. A collection of theater writings—criticism and comment from 1964 to 1975.

Kleb, William. "Sam Shepard's *Inacoma* at the Magic Theatre." *Theater* 9 (Fall 1977): 1. Watching Shepard direct a collective workshop exercise based on the case of Karen Quinlan.

Lahr, John. "Arthur Kopit's *Indians*: Dramatizing National Amnesia." *Up Against the Fourth Wall.* New York: Grove Press, 1969. Critique of *Indians*, relating it to the Vietnam War.

_____. *Astonish Me.* New York: Viking, 1973. Essays on theater. *Operation Sidewinder* essay of particular interest.

Levi-Strauss, Claude. *Myth and Meaning.* New York: Schocken Books, 1979. In five lectures prepared for radio, the French anthropologist explores the nature and role of myth in human history.

Little, Stuart W. *Off Broadway: The Prophetic Theater.* New York: Coward, McCann, & Geoghegan, Inc., 1972. Documentary history of Off Broadway from 1952 to 1972.

Murch, Anne. "Genet-Triana-Kopit: Ritual as 'Danse Macabre.'" *Modern Drama* 15 (March 1973): 369–81. Discussion of *Chamber Music*.

New Yorker, May 11, 1968. Unsigned review of *Red Cross*.

New York Times, January 13, 1964. Kopit angrily denouncing the University of Minnesota for not permitting the public to see a workshop production of *Whores*.

Oppenheim, I., and Ipscio, V. "The Most Promising Playwright in America Today Is Sam Shepard." *Village Voice*, October 23, 1975, pp. 81–82. Interview with Shepard.

Parker, Judith. "A Play Has to Breathe." *Harvard Magazine*, March-April 1979.

Rinear, D. L. "*The Day the Whores Came Out to Play Tennis*: Kopit's Debt to Chekhov." *Today's Speech*, Spring 1974. Shows the thematic and structural relation between the two plays.

Rosen, Carol. "Sam Shepard's Angel City: A Movie for the Stage." *Modern Drama* 22 (Spring 1979): 39–46. Excellent interpretation of the play.

Secrest, Meryle. Interview in *Washington Post*, April 20, 1969. Sets forth Kopit's feeling about the nature of language.

Stambolian, George. "Shepard's *Mad Dog Blues*: A Trip through Popular Culture." *Journal of Popular Culture* 7 (Spring 1974): 776–86.

Stasio, Marilyn. "An Outlaw Comes Home." *After Dark*, January 1980. An overview of Shepard's plays, stressing their unifying theme—the war between father and son.

Szilassy, Zoltan. "Yankee Burlesque or Metaphysical Farce." *Hungarian Studies in English XI*. Debrecen 1979. Critique of *Oh Dad, Poor Dad*.

Taylor, Russell. "Kopit Goes West." *Plays and Players* 15 (1968). Review of London production of *Indians*.

Topor, Tom. Interview with Kopit in *New York Post*, February 1, 1979.

Vermeulen, Michael. "Sam Shepard: Yes, Yes, Yes." *Esquire*, February 1980. Interesting discussion of *Suicide in B Flat*.

Wellworth, George. *The Theater of Protest and Paradox*. New York: New York University Press, 1964. Reports early critical interest in Kopit's *Oh Dad, Poor Dad*.

White, Michael. "Underground 'Landscapes.' " *Guardian*, February 21, 1974. Interview with Shepard in British paper.

Winters, Linda. *Chicago Tribune*, January 6, 1974. Review of *Tooth of Crime*.

Index

Adamov, Arthur, 74, 76–77
American Place Theatre, 11, 16,
  29, 64, 127

Beck, Julian, 118, 124, 126
Beckett, Samuel, 9, 14, 29, 40, 68,
  73; *Endgame*, 68, 69, 77; *Waiting
  for Godot*, 78
Brecht, Bertolt, 17, 18, 29, 30, 32,
  40, 92, 117, 118; *The Threepenny
  Opera*, 7; *The Rise and Fall of the
  City of Mahagonny*, 29; *Jungle of
  Cities*, 29, 30, 31, 32, 33, 39
Brustein, Robert, 111, 120, 127

Cafe Cino, 11, 12
Cafe La Mama, 11, 20, 125
Chaikin, Joseph, 30, 52, 62, 63,
  64, 125
Chekhov, Anton, 84, 85, 117
Chubb, Kenneth, 18
Chelsea Theater, 127
Cino, Joe, 124
Circle in the Square, 114, 115, 116,
  118
Civic Repertory, 113
Cook, Ralph, 9, 19

Dunster House, 67
Durrenmatt, Friedrich, 76
Dylan, Bob, 44

Esslin, Martin, 72, 77

Hambleton, Edward, T., 117
Harvard Dramatic Club, 67
Houghton, Norris, 117

Hughes, Howard, 49
Hughes, Ted, 34

Ionesco, Ernest, 72, 73, 83, 117
Italie, Claude Van, 126

Jacobson, Roman, 107
Johnson, O-Lan, 27, 29
Jones, LeRoi, 14, 127
Judson Poets' Theatre, 11

Kleist, Heinrich von, 76
Kopit, Arthur: American themes,
  88–102; early plays, 66–71;
  Harvard plays, 67–70; language, 69, 70, 104–110; Vietnam as theme, 23, 87, 88, 90,
  102

WORKS
"Across the River and into the
  Jungle," 68
"Aubade," 68
Chamber Music, 68, 78, 80–83,
  105
*The Day the Whores Came Out to
  Play Tennis*, 67, 80, 83–86
"Don Juan in Texas," 67
Indians, 67, 68, 70, 85, 87–102
*Oh Dad, Poor Dad, Mamma's Hung
  You in the Closet and I'm Feelin'
  So Sad*, 66, 70, 72–79
"On the Runway of Life You
  Never Know What's Coming
  Off Next," 67
"The Questioning of Nick," 67
"Sing to Me Through Open
  Windows," 68

"To Dwell in a Palace of
    Strangers," 68
"Vital Matter of Environment,"
    70, 73
Wings, 67, 70, 78, 103—110

Lahr, John, 88, 97
La Mama Experimental Theatre
    Club, 17
La Mama's New Troupe, 19
Levi-Strauss, Claude, 3, 47, 88
Levy, Jacques, 15, 16
Living Theater, 119

Magic Theatre, 51, 64
Malina, Judith, 119
Mallarmé, Stéphane, 33
Manhattan Project, 125
Manhattan Theater Club, 127
Mann, Theodore, 115, 116, 117
Mark Taper Forum, 18

Neighborhood Playhouse, 112
Nerval, Gérard de, 29
New York Shakespeare Festival,
    118, 120—22

O'Horgan, Tom, 17, 19
O'Neill, Eugene, 112; The Iceman
    Cometh, 115; Long Day's Journey
    into Night, 79
Ontological-Hysterical Theater,
    125, 126
Open Theatre, 52, 125, 126

Page, Geraldine, 116, 118
Papp, Joseph, 47, 120—24
Performance Group, 125
Phoenix Theatre, 66, 116, 117—18
Provincetown Players, 112
Public Theatre, 62, 122—23

Pulitzer Prize, 53

Quintero, Jose, 114, 116, 117

Rimbaud, Arthur, 32
Rolling Thunder Revue, 44
Roundabout Theater, 127
Royal Shakespeare Company, 87

Schechner, Richard, 5, 43, 124,
    125
Shepard, Sam: American family, 1,
    9, 48, 53; betrayal of American
    dream, 1, 7, 49, 50, 54, 56—58;
    boyhood, 2; childhood, 47; early
    employment, 2—3; early plays,
    9—25; English years, 27—44;
    idiom, 1, 3, 6, 40; language, 10,
    44, 46, 62; music, 7, 28, 46,
    62; myth, 1, 2, 4, 18, 28, 46,
    48, 54—56; return to U.S.,
    45—65; women characters, 8,
    40, 50—51, 59—61

WORKS
Action, 42, 51
Angel City, 4, 7, 45—46, 51
Back Dog Beast Bait, 28
Buried Child, 7, 18, 19, 48,
    53—61
Chicago, 11—12
Cowboy Mouth, 7, 27, 28, 29
Cowboys, 9, 28
Cowboys No. 2, 18—19, 28
Curse of the Starving Class, 7, 9,
    18, 47—49, 53
Dog, 11
Forensic and the Navigators, 19, 52
4H Club, 14
Fourteen Hundred Thousand, 14
Geography of a Horse Dreamer,
    43—44

The Holy Ghostly, 19, 28
Icarus's Mother, 12—15, 45
In a Coma, 51—52, 62
Killer Head, 64
La Turista, 16—17
The Mad Dog Blues, 4, 7, 8
Melodrama Play, 17—18
Operation Sidewinder, 22—25, 27
Red Cross, 15
Rock Garden, 9, 11, 48, 58
Rolling Thunder Log Book, 44
"Visualization, Language and the
    Inner Library," 62
Seduced, 49—51
Suicide in B Flat, 7, 18, 46—47
Tongues, 18, 48, 62—65
Savage / Love, 62, 64
The Tooth of Crime, 6, 7, 17, 18,
    19, 27—41
The Unseen Hand, 20, 28
Up to Thursday, 11

Smith, Patti, 27, 29, 30

Terry, Magan, 126
Theater Guild, 112
Theater of the Ridiculous, 125
Theater 65, 11, 14
Theatre Genesis, 9, 11, 19
Theatre of the Absurd, 40, 42, 43,
    68, 72, 73, 75, 77, 78

Verlaine, Paul, 32
Villon, François, 29
Vivian Beaumont Repertory
    Theatre, 22, 122—23

Washington Square Players, 112
Weill, Kurt, 30
Weiss, Peter, 80
Williams, Tennessee, *Summer and
    Smoke*, 115
Wylie, Philip, 75

Yale Repertory Theatre, 47, 103

DATE DUE
